# Soilfree Growing & Decorating Ideas

This book could just as easily be called "After the Party's Over." The party we're referring to, of course, is the Deco Plant Party at which you were first introduced to the Soilfree Deco Plantsystem. There you learned the fundamentals of growing beautiful, healthy plants in a Nutrient Solution rather than soil. It all looks so easy and fun . . . and it is.

Just in case you missed a point or two, our first chapter reviews all those basics. Then we go on to tell everything else you'll ever need to know about the Deco Plantsystem, show more than four dozen other Deco Plants you might want to consider, and spark your decorating imagination with page after page of plant-tastic ideas.

The information on how to keep your plants green and growing, stamping out pest problems, giving your plants a fresh start, the plant identification section and the plant decorating ideas have been specifically prepared for you by the editors of *Better Homes and Gardens®* magazine.

Photography: Bob Hawks
*(except where noted)*

the plant party people®

deco plants
company®

A DIVISION OF RALSTON PURINA COMPANY ®

# Contents

4

# CHAPTER 1
# Welcome to the wonderful world of Deco Plants

Have you ever stood by helplessly while a favorite house-plant turned a sickly yellow, withered and died? Perhaps you'd been giving the victim too much water . . . or too little . . . over- or underfeeding . . . or maybe insects or disease ruined its roots. Some of the worst problems a plant can have occur underground, where you can't see them until it's too late.

Deco's Plantsystem reduces soil-related problems by eliminating soil. Instead, plants grow in a bed of Living Stones®, nourished by a liquid Nutrient Solution that's scientifically formulated for optimum health and growth.

These are the essentials of the Soilfree Deco Plantsystem, but they're only part of a remarkable story. Join us, now, on this guided tour of the wonderful world of Deco.

5

*Photograph: Tom Monday*

# Quality plants need the best possible start

### Cuttings from the tropical jungles of Latin America

Borneo, the West Indies, Malaysia, Brazil, South Africa, India, China . . . today's houseplants have their origins in exotic places around the globe, most of them tropical or semitropical regions near the equator. Many Deco Plants begin life in almost identical environments—on plantations like this one in Guatemala (above). Here workers take cuttings from only the healthiest, hardiest parents.

### Packed, shipped, stored and checked with the utmost of care

The cuttings set out on a long journey from their native jungles to your home. First stop: a refrigerated storeroom in the Deco Plants greenhouse at Apopka, Florida. As the cuttings are unpacked, technicians painstakingly scrutinize each of them for any evidence of disease, insects, or other problems. The shipment shown in the photograph at right came from Costa Rica, in Central America.

*Photographs: Jim Hedrich, Hedrich Bles*

## Roots develop in beds of water and crushed stone . . . the soilfree way

Cuttings that pass their "physicals" get a chance to sprout the unique root systems they'll need as Deco Plants. Propped in wet crushed stone (above), they learn to live on a liquid diet. Conventional, soil-grown plants are sometimes rooted this way, too—but their root systems have to change after they've been potted. Most Deco Plants begin their lives in crushed stone and grow the right roots from the very start. All receive close, personal attention at every stage of growth.

## When fledgling plants come of age, each wins Living Stones and a pot of its own

Once a young plantlet's roots reach a certain size, it's checked for problems yet again. Then nimble, experienced fingers arrange roots of the healthiest plants in baskets of Deco's Living Stones. Note in the photograph at right that each container already has a Visual Moisture Level Indicator—so the plant can easily signal its water and nutrient needs for the rest of its life.

7

Welcome to the wonderful
world of Deco Plants
*Continued*

# 13 Acres of Deco Plants under one roof...

and not a speck of soil in sight! In Deco Plants' immense Apopka, Florida, greenhouse—the largest facility of its kind in North America—thousands upon thousands of newly potted beauties bask in a nearly perfect hydroculture environment.

Here young plants wait for periods ranging from several weeks to several months before technicians deem them mature and luxuriant enough for your home. Then the now-seasoned Deco Plants get one last checkup, and board special refrigerated trucks for shipment to Deco Centers throughout the United States.

Shipping can be tough on a plant, but kid-glove packing and handling procedures—plus the soilfree system itself—assure that each Deco Plant arrives at your home fresh and ready to grow.

We'll get into the care and feeding of your plant a little later . . . but first, let's drop in on a plant party and see why we've chosen this fun, friendly way to explain the magic of Deco Plants.

*Photograph:
Jim Hedrich,
Hedrich Belssing*

## From a Deco Plant Party...
## to you and your home

**Remember the Deco Consultant who first told you about the Soilfree Plantsystem?**

Weren't you impressed by her warmth and enthusiasm? Good feelings just seem to come naturally when you're meeting new people, demonstrating a delightful product, making parties happen . . . and earning good money as an independent business person. Best of all, each consultant sets her own pace and schedule, so there is time for family as well as career.

## How can I become a hostess . . . or a Deco Consultant?

Actually, the best way to find out if you'd really enjoy working as a consultant is to try a turn or two as a hostess first. Just let your consultant know you'd like to give a Deco Party. She'll arrange a date with you and get you started.

Parties, incidentally, are the key to the way Deco products are marketed. They offer a fun way to sell plants and accessories, of course. Just as importantly, they give the hostess and consultant an opportunity to book other parties. And it's bookings—the more of them the better—that multiply the possibilities for future sales.

What are the requirements for consultants? A love for people and plants, mainly. You don't need any experience or initial investment. Again, for more details, ask your consultant.

## What about the hostess of a Deco Plant Party?

She might be an old friend of the consultant—or a new one who attended a previous plant party and got caught up in the fun of it all. Having a Deco Party offers a marvelous opportunity to gather everyone you've been meaning to see more of—neighbors, relatives, co-workers, whomever. And as a hostess you also earn gift credits or specials for Deco Plant sales and other parties that result from your party.

## But isn't a Deco Party a lot of work?

Not at all. You'll want to tidy up the house and make some simple refreshments, of course. But your Deco Consultant is an expert on parties. She'll help you draw up a guest list, make the invitations, welcome guests, and do all she can to create a relaxed, pressure-free feeling in your home.

# Now, meet the Deco Plantsystem family.

Familiarize yourself with the few simple components and accessories in this family portrait, and your plants never again need to worry about over- or underwatering and over- or underfeeding.

Let's start at the lower left-hand corner of the opposite page, with the boxed *Plantset* kit you might buy to start your own cuttings or pot an existing plant. It has all the elements of the Soilfree Deco Plantsystem—but not the plant itself.

Arrayed in front of the boxes, from left to right, are: the container's outer, decorative *shell*—available in four sizes and many colors; the brown inner *Planting Basket* and its floating *Visual Moisture Level Indicator*; a bottle of the *Nutrient* you mix with water; and a package of Deco's *Living Stones*.

Those two L-shaped items on the right are optional *wall brackets* that hold 9-inch and 4- to 7-inch pots; they're not part of the basic Plantset kit. Neither is the *leather hanger* at upper left; it hangs one plant, as shown, and you can fit in a second above the brass ring.

You can buy Deco components separately, too, as pictured below. The Nutrient comes in 2- and 16-ounce bottles. Since you add only a teaspoon to two quarts of water, the larger size lasts a long time.

Living Stones are packaged according to the size of pot used. Shown here are the four sizes, with their corresponding containers. From the bottom up, the pots measure 4, 5, 7, and 9 inches in diameter. Note that color choices vary from size to size, and that you can also pot a Deco Plant in a larger floor container. Just use the *Visual Moisture Level Indicator*—21 centimeters high—standing amongst the pots (below).

These are the basics, but Deco researchers are continually developing other products to make the Soilfree Deco Plantsystem even easier or more versatile. Your consultant will know about any new items not shown here.

13

# Why does the Soilfree Plantsystem work so well?

Growing plants in water dates back centuries, and many a modern day commercial grower raises bumper crops of vegetables—scientifically and under perfectly controlled conditions—without soil. Until recently, though, hydroculture techniques were simply too tricky for amateurs to bother with.

The Soilfree Deco Plantsystem changes all that. For a clear understanding of how it works, consider the important jobs a plant's roots have to do. First, as you might have guessed, they provide support—feet, of sorts, that the plant can stand on.

Even more important, the roots are also responsible for taking in nourishment. Using a process which works much like a drinking straw, the roots absorb water and send it upstairs to the leaves.

Plant roots require water and fertilizer, of course . . . but did you know they also need air? Keep roots constantly wet—without oxygen or air—and they'll begin to rot.

You only have to look at nature to realize soil makes an excellent growing medium. There's a big difference, though, between a whole yard full of earth and just a few ounces in an ordinary pot. Outdoors, excess water runs off or seeps deep into the ground, so the roots get a chance to dry out periodically. Worms and some insects help, too, by aerating the soil with their burrows.

In a pot, though, an overabundance of moisture has no place to go. Water too much or too often and roots get waterlogged. The same goes for fertilizer. This is why it's so easy to literally drown an ordinary houseplant with kindness. You can't *see* just how much water remains underground—and because root systems vary in the rate at which they absorb water, different plants have to be watered on different schedules. Just keeping track of it all can get confusing.

Not with the Soilfree Deco Plantsystem. It takes all the guesswork out of watering and feeding because you can precisely regulate each plant's intake. Much of the credit goes to Deco's Living Stones, a lightweight, man-made aggregate that gives roots clean, stable support, and lets them get just the amounts of air and moisture they need.

Deco's Nutrient Solution also makes plant feeding much easier and surer. This mild, balanced fertilizer provides everything plants need for healthy growth. Just add one teaspoon to two quarts of water, then pour slowly over the Living Stones.

**With square, two-part Deco containers** like the one above, pour Nutrient Solution gradually until the nutrient level nears the top edge of the little window in the bottom reservoir. Don't refill until the level drops to the window's lower edge— usually 10 to 15 days.

**Visual Moisture Level Indicators,** such as the one at left, have a red pointer that floats in a plastic sleeve. Add Nutrient Solution until the red indicator stem is at top of gauge. Don't refill until the red indicator has sunk almost out of sight.

You can adapt the Soilfree Deco Plantsystem to other containers, too. Just drop in the inner Planting Basket, as shown below. Be sure, though, that the pots you select are nonporous plastic, glass or glazed ceramic—and have no drainage holes.

## More about how the Plantsystem works

Square, two-part Deco containers, such as the one shown on the preceding page are goofproof. Add too much Nutrient Solution and the bottom reservoir will simply overflow. It *is* possible to overfill a round, Deco pot—but then the Moisture Level Indicator will rise right through the top of its plastic sleeve and let you know you've made a mistake.

With either container, pour the solution a little at a time, then pause to let it trickle through the Living Stones before you take a reading. If you do happen to add too much, just lift out the Planting Basket and pour off the excess solution.

Don't be too eager to top up the moisture level again, either. Always let it drop to the lowest point first. This gives the roots exactly the balance of air and Nutrient they need for healthy growth. (If, however, you'll be away from home for a week or two, fill to the top—regardless of what the indicator says—and your Deco Plant will take care of itself while you're gone.)

**The container below shows how moisture clings** to Deco's Living Stones. Notice that only those at the very bottom are actually underwater; capillary action—the tendency of a liquid to seek the smallest opening—causes the Nutrient Solution to pull its way up between the spaces among the stones. Note the resulting irregular water surface.

Plants differ quite a bit in the amounts of moisture they need. Thirsty specimens send down deep roots and drink as much of it as they can; others are practically teetotalers, so they develop shallow root systems.

This is what makes watering *soil-grown* houseplants so confusing. Some like short sips every day or so. Some prefer only a thorough weekly wetting. A few, such as cacti, are like miniature camels and thrive in long, dry spells.

Varying humidity levels in your home obviously make a difference, too. It's easier to drown an ordinary plant in muggy weather, or parch it under arid winter conditions. And since most plants need to rest every so often, they require less water during dormant periods.

The Soilfree Deco Plantsystem automatically compensates for all these variables. Each plant's roots help themselves to just as much moisture and Nutrient as they need. And as the fluid level drops, they also get enough air to prevent root rot. You'll notice that some Deco Plants like life on the dry side and need watering less often.

Although the Soilfree Deco Plantsystem takes most of the guesswork out of watering and feeding, you'll want to check the following pages for many more ideas for keeping all your Deco Plants happy and healthy.

**Want to use the Deco Plantsystem with a really large,** floorstanding plant? King-size Moisture Level Indicators—21 centimeters high—let you turn almost any pot into a Deco container. You have to dispense with the inner Planting Basket, of course.

# CHAPTER 2
## How to keep your plants green & growing

The moment a Deco Plant arrives in your home, you have some important decisions to make. "Where shall I put it?" is usually the first. And how you answer that question makes all the difference in your plant's new world.

You've probably heard about talking to plants. . . they really do seem to enjoy it. But did you know they can also talk back? Locate one where it gets too much light, for example—or not enough humidity—and it'll tell you.

This chapter spells out all the basics you need to know about providing a healthy, happy environment for your plants—and how you can recognize any complaints your plants might have. Then we share some beauty secrets you can use to keep your plants looking their best.

19

# First, learn these basic facts of light

**Does your plant need direct sun?** Bright, medium or low light? Here only the Jade Plant gets a place in the sun. But the Ming Tree, African Violet and Zebra Plant like bright spots near windows—as does the Schefflera on the floor. Medium-light lovers include the Danica Ivy by the lamp, as well as the Warnecki Dracaena behind the sofa. Next to them at far right are a Palm and a Silver King Evergreen. It will grow in low light, as will the Snake Plant, Heart-leaf Philodendron and Ribbon Plant in corner, English Ivy in foreground.

Plants knew about solar energy long before the rest of us. They depend on it for their very lives. Give any plant less sunlight than it needs—or more than it can handle—and you'll soon have problems.

To understand why, let's begin by looking at how the growing process works. It requires four key elements—*nutrients* to feed the plant; *water* to carry the nutrients through roots and stems; *air* to help the chlorophyll-containing leaves turn the nutrients and water into sugars and starches. . . and *light* to make it all happen! The scientific name for all this, *photosynthesis*, literally translates as "putting together with light."

The Soilfree Plantsystem provides your Deco Plant with a reservoir of water and nutrients it can draw on for healthy, scientifically controlled growth. Your home already has an abundance of air. (Temperature and humidity make a difference here, but more about that later.) It's up to you, though, to shed just the right amount of light on the subject.

Plants vary widely in their appetites for light. To help you find a good spot for your particular Deco Plant, we have identified each one according to whether it favors low, medium or bright conditions, or direct sun (see pages 52 to 73). Check these guidelines.

**Low light** prevails in areas more than six feet from a non-shaded east, west or south window. Don't confuse low light with *no* light. Generally, if no shadows are cast during the day, there's not enough light to grow anything well. Realize that although a number of plants can tolerate dim conditions, most do a lot better in medium light.

**Medium light** is what you get at three to six feet from unshaded windows. As with other light level ranges given here, situate plants a little closer to east or west windows, farther away from south windows. The list of plants that prefer medium light goes on and on—Corn Plant, Marble Queen, Peperomia, Red and Green Emeralds, most Ivies and Yucca are just a few.

**Bright light** falls within three feet of any but a north window, and is a must for plants—especially flowering types—that simply won't grow under any other condition. During the dark days of winter, you might also want to use a bright-light area as a hospital for others that aren't doing well elsewhere. Most colorful plants—such as the Hoya, Zebra and Peace Lily—as well as some others (Ming Aralia and Schefflera) favor bright light. The brighter the exposure, without direct sun, the richer their colors. African Violets need bright light to induce—and maintain—flowering.

**Direct sun** suits only a very few houseplants—and even most of these shouldn't get more than five hours of sun a day. Otherwise, their leaves may burn—especially if they're not adapted to direct sun slowly. Sheer draperies help diffuse light from windows that face into the sun. Sunburning can be a special problem in the wintertime, when trees outside have lost their leaves or when intense rays are reflected from snow. Windowpanes also can magnify the sun's rays.

If you have a photographic light meter, you can more precisely measure these levels in *footcandles*. Hold the meter near the plant's leaf surfaces, take several incident light readings at different times of day and average them. Low light falls in the 25- to 50-footcandle range; medium, 50 to 100 footcandles; high, 100 to 200.

Fortunately, many Deco Plants do nicely under a variety of different light conditions. And even if you have your heart set on a location that's too dark for your pride and joy, there are several strategies you can employ. One is to simply move the plant to a brighter spot every day and leave it there for at least half a day. Watch out for direct sun, though. Leaves accustomed to low light will burn in almost no time.

Plant rental firms—outfits that often supply the luxuriant greenery you see in public places—sometimes resort to another trick. They provide two specimens of the same plant, then switch them back and forth between low- and better-light areas. Rotate them weekly—or more often—to keep both healthy.

If you'd rather not play either of these musical plant games, consider supplementing inadequate natural light with artificial illumination from grow-lights or reading lamps. More about this on page 25.

**What happens when a plant doesn't get enough light?** Nothing at first. Most have food reserves that let them ride out long shady periods. After a while, however, new growth comes in spindly, with smaller leaves. Lower leaves yellow and die. Flowering plants stop blooming, and 'colorful' plants lose their brilliance. If you spot these symptoms, try a brighter location. Soon the plant will perk up.

**The anemic-looking Red Emerald Philodendron** at left didn't get the medium to high light levels needed for good growth. Notice how stunted it appears compared to the healthy specimen at right.

**What happens when there's too much light?** Plants acclimated to shady conditions can quickly grow out of bounds in brighter areas. To get them under control again, cut back foliage, as explained on page 31, then relocate the plant to a dimmer setting.

Realize, too, that you could shock a light-starved specimen by suddenly moving it close to a window. Plants don't like abrupt changes in their environments, so go easy. To learn about the symptoms and solutions for sunburning, see below.

**Why do some houseplants grow one-sided?** Plants are *phototropic*, which means they love light as much as kids love cookies—and like kids, they'll go through any contortions to get what they want. In many rooms, natural light comes from a single direction, and you'll

# Light facts:
## Problems & solutions

find plants leaning and even stretching toward a window. To keep its growth symmetrical, simply rotate the plant a quarter turn or so every few days. You may need to prune foliage, too; see page 31.

**How can I help my plant keep its shape?** Again, take advantage of its fondness for light by favoring the parts you'd like to develop. If you want a plant to climb, for example, provide strings or a trellis that get good light. Suspend a hanging container high in a window and foliage will happily cascade over the sides.

Below and on the opposite page are photographs of five light-sick plants. Problems include sunburn, too much light, failure to turn plants, too little light, failure to bloom and a few others. Compare them with any you might be worrying about. Then follow our suggestions for making your plant look well again.

## Problem:

Direct sun has caused leaves closest to the window to turn yellow, then brown. You may see spots on some leaves—or scorched edges and tips, such as those on this sunburn case. Burned tissues make it impossible for leaves to synthesize food, so eventually the plant takes on a faded, bleached look.

## Solution:

Moving to a shadier spot will soon set things right—or you might consider filtering strong sunlight through sheer draperies. Damaged growth won't repair itself, so you may as well remove it. With broadleaf plants like this one, you can simply snip away scorched portions of each leaf. Chilling may cause similar symptoms. More on page 27.

## Problem:

All leaves face in the same direction, and the entire plant may be leaning toward a window or other light source. Notice that with this Hawaiian Schefflera, the stems that connect leaves to the stalks have also grown abnormally long and the leaves themselves look somewhat pale and stunted.

## Solution:

Plants shape themselves according to where light is coming from. To even up growth, turn them regularly—at least once a week. Also, this Schefflera hasn't been getting the medium-to-high light levels it needs for healthy growth—hence the elongated stems and pasty appearance. It should be situated near a window, but not in direct sun.

## Problem:

Growth is even, but the stems have become extremely elongated and drooping. Those on this dejected-looking Umbrella Tree (Schefflera) are so fragile that merely touching one could cause it to break away from its stalk. Eventually, just the weight of the leaves will snap off stems.

## Solution:

Again, too little light is the culprit. This particular species must get at least four hours of high (but not direct) light every day. Move the plant right up next to a window, but watch out for those delicate stems when you do this. Be sure plant doesn't touch windowpane. The stems won't shrink, of course, but in time new growth will come in shorter and sturdier.

## Problem:

Long, leggy growth and dwarfed leaves—many of them turning yellow—make it hard to even recognize this woebegone Green Emerald Philodendron. . . yet another victim of light starvation! Though they may look to be at death's door, plants can limp along in this condition for months—even years.

## Solution:

Start by radically trimming back the worst growth and gradually providing more light. Green Emeralds want medium to high levels and won't settle for anything less. In some cases you might be better off to take a healthy-looking stem cutting, destroy the rest of the plant, and start all over again, as shown on page 45.

## Problem:

Blooming plants must have very bright indirect light—and sometimes even a touch of direct sun, but only a few minutes—if they're to reward you with blossoms. In lower light conditions they'll rarely if ever flower, and stems will grow long and spindly. This lackluster African Violet is a case in point.

## Solution:

Cut away weak foliage and gradually give the plant lots of strong, bright light (but no direct sun for African Violets, please). Healthy specimens grow compact and bloom throughout the entire year. If your plants just can't seem to get enough sunlight—no matter where you put them—try brightening their lives with artificial light. To learn how, turn the page.

Once you've begun to appreciate the many advantages and features of the Soilfree Deco Plantsystem—and the luxuriant foliage it yields—gardening with artificial light offers a logical next step. Hydroculture lets you exactly control the nutrients your plant receives; color-balanced fluorescent tubes or incandescent bulbs (grow-lights) do the same with its light levels.

You can use special fluorescent tubes or bulbs specifically made for growing plants. However, for most homeowner purposes, color-balanced tubes or bulbs are not really necessary if the plant receives any natural light at all. In that situation, regular fluorescents or incandescent bulbs are both acceptable.

Use artificial lights to augment natural light in a dim corner, extend daylight hours for sun-lovers, or bring plants to areas of your home where you've never been able to grow things before. You might even want to consider setting up an artificially lighted plant resort (a basement table will do) where winter-weary stragglers can go for restorative vacations.

**What are grow-lights?** What we think of as "white" sunlight actually includes every color in the rainbow. Plants don't use all of these wavelengths, however—they use mainly those we see as blue at one end of the spectrum and those we perceive as red at the other. Ordinary incandescent bulbs give lots of red waves, but little blue; fluorescents produce lots of blue light, but almost no red. Grow-lights give off both reds and blues, but none of the wavelengths in between.

Because they emit very few of the midrange waves, grow-lights may appear dimmer than ordinary bulbs or tubes, and they glow with an eerie pinkish or bluish hue. Not only do plants thrive under this light, they look better, too. Greens seem lusher, richer and darker; some flowers literally glow with vibrant colors.

**How much artificial light do I need?** The answer depends upon your plants' natural light preferences. Deco Plants that require only low, natural light levels

# Light facts: Growing under artificial lights

can do nicely at three feet from a 40-watt fluorescent light or the same distance from a 100-watt incandescent bulb. Medium-light levels occur at two feet from a 40-watt fluorescent tube and three feet from a 150-watt incandescent bulb. Plants that demand high levels of natural light should be situated one foot from a 40-watt fluorescent light, three feet from a 300-watt incandescent source.

Another way to compute artificial light levels is in watts per square foot. Most foliage plants will do well if they get 15 watts per square foot at a distance of 15 inches from a fluorescent source; flowering plants need 20 watts per square foot, at a distance of 10 inches. Incandescent bulbs, though they're as effective as fluorescents, pose a special problem. Because they emit heat that could burn foliage, you should keep them at least two feet away.

Note, too, that plants placed directly under lamps receive more light than those at the edges. And bear in mind that these figures are only rules of thumb. You may need to experiment with different distances to find the one your plants like best.

**Like people, plants need sleep**. . . eight to ten hours of it every day. So establish a regular schedule of turning on lights for 14 to 16 hours, then giving your Deco Plants their beauty rest. To assure that you don't inadvertently keep them in the dark—or the light—for too long, connect the lights to an inexpensive timing device.

Ideally, some houseplants need never see the natural light of day—but while you're experimenting, rotate yours from artificial to natural light on a weekly basis. Keep an eye out, too, for the poor light symptoms shown on the preceding pages. A plant that grows leggy or spindly may need a higher intensity light—or more of the real thing.

**Where's the best place for grow-lights?** Locate them almost anywhere you like, provided you maintain the distances from foliage recommended above. The photograph on the opposite page shows one popular, bookshelf arrangement. It uses special fixtures that stand on legs. Standard fluorescent lights (with plant tubes) could also have been fastened to the shelves' undersides, and you can hang fluorescent or incandescent fixtures over tables, mount them on walls, or—for maximum flexibility—use some floor standing lamps. Whatever setup you decide on, just be sure it lets you adjust the distance between the light source and your plants so you can vary intensity levels for optimum growth.

## These plants grow well under lights

| | | |
|---|---|---|
| African Violet | Heart-leaf Philodendron | Silver King Evergreen |
| Chinese Evergreen | | |
| | Snake Plant | English Ivy |
| Ribbon Plant | | |
| | Silver Evergreen | |
| Parlor Palm | | |
| | Prayer Plant | |

# Watch for water and temperature problems

You needn't worry about overwatering or overfeeding a Deco Plant, but the chemical balance of the water itself can cause problems with some species.

Burned leaf tips on this plant resulted from a high level of fluoride in its water. Peace Lilies, Yuccas and most Dracaenas are also fluoride-prone. If the fluoride in your water exceeds .5 parts per million (your community water department can tell you this), switch to rainwater, bottled water or some other chemical-free source.

Very soft water, on the other hand, may not have the calcium a plant needs—resulting in foliage that's pale or off-color. If this is the case at your house, use spring water or well water.

## Problem:

White residue accumulates on top of the Living Stones. Lower leaves begin to brown at their edges, scorch, droop and drop off.

## Solution:

Feeding and watering any plant builds up white, crystalized salts. Accumulated salts near the roots make it much more difficult for them to absorb nutrients. To keep your plants' roots drinking freely, flush away the salts every three months with lukewarm water—a task called *leaching*.

Leaching *soil* plants is a messy proposition, which probably explains why few people ever bother to do it. With Deco Plants, it's a snap. Just hold the plant under a faucet, as explained below.

## Problem:

What's the best way to get rid of built-up salt residue on Living Stones?

## Solution:

Lift out the inner Planting Basket and set it under the faucet in a sink or—for larger plants—your bathtub. Turn on the faucet gently, so water pressure doesn't churn the Living Stones out of their container. Run lukewarm water through the stones for a few minutes, then shut it off. After the basket has drained, replace it in the outer container and add fresh Nutrient Solution.

To leach a square, two-part Deco container, remove the upper section and run water through it. Rinse out the base, too. While you're leaching a plant, give its leaves an invigorating shower (see page 30).

## Problem:

**Plants near windows begin to shrivel during cold or hot weather.**

## Solution:

Houseplants just can't handle the drastic extremes of hot and cold that sometimes occur near windows. During the day, glass magnifies and traps the sun's heat. At night, temperatures might be cooler here than anywhere else in the room.

If a plant starts to suffer, move it back from the window right away. And never imprison a plant between draperies and the glass—day or night.

## Problem:

**Leaves continue to drop off a plant that's stationed near a door.**

## Solution:

Right next to the front entry might seem a congenial spot for this *Ficus benjamina* to welcome visitors—but every time a guest arrives, the plant gets buffeted by a blast of cold air. Even interior doors can sometimes cause problems. Opening and closing them creates drafts and puts the plant under stress from erratically fluctuating temperature and moisture conditions. More on the following page.

## Problem:

**Your Deco Plant seems to be losing its leaves from the bottom up.**

## Solution:

Again, a draft—this time a hot one from an air register—is putting the foliage under a great deal of stress. Leave this Rubber Tree in its present location much longer and it'll die of heat prostration.

One early sign of a draft problem: The plant seems thirsty and needs Nutrient Solution much more often than others. Humidity levels are usually lower near air registers, too.

## Problem:

**Some plants like cool temperatures, so why not set one by an air conditioner?**

## Solution:

Aralias, such as this Chicken Gizzard, are especially sensitive to drafts—and rapidly shed their leaves in response. Also, temperatures and humidity levels fluctuate more near air conditioners because their cooling units are continually cycling on and off. Move this plant to a calm location and it'll soon regain its composure.

## Four ways to boost humidity

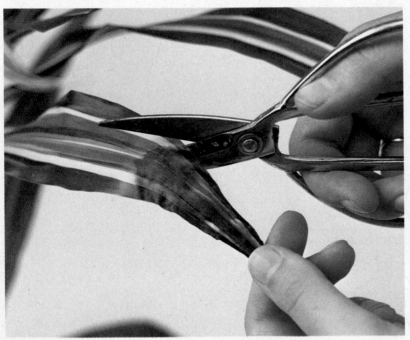

Since Deco plants grow in water, why should lack of humidity ever be a problem? The reason has to do with the way leaves work. Their job, remember, is to synthesize sugar and starch from nutrients the roots send up. In the process of doing this, they give off oxygen and moisture. Dry air absorbs the moisture too quickly, the entire cycle speeds up, and the plant doesn't get enough time to properly digest its food.

Tropical creatures that they are, houseplants are accustomed to much more humidity than people prefer—and dry winter air sometimes makes even *us* uncomfortable. Air conditioning, which dehumidifies as well as cools, also drinks up plant moisture.

The first signs of a humidity problem show up at leaf tips, which begin to brown like the one at left. Snip these off, then take measures to increase humidity in the plant's immediate vicinity.

Many plant lovers do this by misting foliage daily. Misting helps somewhat, but dry air can soak up that extra moisture in almost no time. In a greenhouse, for example, plants are misted automatically every 15 minutes.

The photos which follow show more practical methods of giving leaves the moisture they need for health and happiness.

*Photograph: William Hopkins*

**1. If a new transplant begins to wilt, mist it regularly for the first couple of weeks.**

Misting does help fresh plantings get used to their new environments. Group them together to help retain moisture, and spray three or four times a day—or whenever leaves seem to be wilting.

Always use room-temperature water, and don't mist after sundown. Instead, give the leaves a chance to dry off so they don't remain damp overnight and risk attacks of fungus or mildew.

An excellent alternative—one that works for mature plants as well—is to treat them to a vaporizing humidifier. Set it nearby, and operate it continually during dry periods. Check the humidifier's water level frequently; you'll be surprised at how often it needs to be refilled.

## 2. Provide moisture for parched plants by setting them in a saucer filled with pebbles and water.

This African Violet takes advantage of water's tendency to evaporate in dry air. The container sits in a dish atop an inch or two of small, washed river pebbles. Water was added until its level came to just below the surface of the upper pebbles. As the water evaporates, it boosts humidity in the air directly around the plant.

The round and irregular pebbles act much the same way as do the Living Stones in a Deco container, helping to bring moisture to the surface via capillary action. This results in much more surface evaporation than if you were to use water alone. To adapt this technique for a grouping of plants, use a large tray instead of the saucer.

## 3. Or, simply set the entire Deco container directly in water for a similar effect.

You won't add as much humidity to the air as you would if the dish also had pebbles in it, but this method will help a struggling plant survive dry spells. Of course, you can't use a lot of water in a deep dish or the Deco container may tip.

Humidity levels fluctuate drastically throughout the year, mainly because air simply can't hold as much moisture at lower temperatures as it can at higher ones. This explains why winter air—which has been heated but not greatly humidified by your furnace—often has a relative humidity of only 20 to 30%. And that's far too dry for plants accustomed to tropical environments in the 50 to 80% range. Keep a close watch on your plants as seasons change.

## Before you leave for a vacation, put your plants in plastic-bag greenhouses.

They'll enjoy a pleasant holiday, too, in their sealed mini-ecologies. First, top up each with Nutrient Solution (regardless, in this case, of what the moisture level indicator says). Then carefully lower the container into the bag. Now blow up the bag and tie the top. Your plant will get all the air, moisture and food it needs for the next couple of weeks.

Take care, though, that plant leaves don't touch the bag itself. Water collecting on their edges can cause rot. If blowing up the bag doesn't provide clearance, slip small stakes or pieces of coat hanger into the Living Stones to prop bag away from leaves. Place the plant out of direct sun, and don't let indoor temperatures exceed 85 degrees while you're gone.

# ...and looking their very best

A well-groomed plant feels the same boost in spirits you do after a lingering bath or a trip to the hair stylist. Plant grooming is fun, too, because you see the results of your handiwork right away.

Insecticide residue and water spots wipe off easily with a damp cloth, as shown at right—or just rub the foliage gently between your thumb and fingers. Always support a leaf while you rub.

Polishing with a moist cloth also gets rid of dust and grime that can clog leaf pores and impede breathing. Don't use anything but water or a mildly soapy solution. Clean African Violets with a soft, dry brush. Never use water or solutions.

*Photograph: William Hopkins*

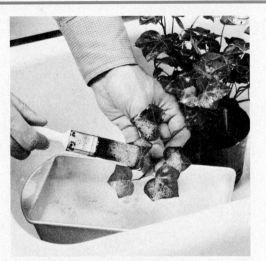

**A soapy bath in a tray of lukewarm water makes sense for smaller-leaf plants such as this ivy.**

Go easy on the soap—just a drop or two of mild dish detergent will do. Swish the leaves around in the solution and use a small brush, sponge or soft cloth to brush away any residue that remains. Rinse with water, then let the leaves and Planting Basket dry for an hour or so before you reassemble the Deco container. As you replenish the Nutrient Solution, you'll almost be able to hear your plant singing its thanks.

Periodic washing not only makes plants look brighter and greener, but it also wards off attacks by bugs and diseases and gives you a chance to thoroughly check for any problems that might be developing. Pages 20 to 29 and 32 to 41 show the symptoms you should be looking for and what to do.

**Or, give your plants a refreshing shower bath in the tub or kitchen sink.**

Again, use lukewarm water—and adjust the pressure so you don't churn the Living Stones out of their container. Spraying promotes the humidity levels most plants crave and leaves them with a healthy glow. Just be sure to let excess water drain before you put the container back together and add Nutrient.

As you give plants their baths, snap or snip off any brown, yellow or unhealthy-looking leaves. Dying foliage robs nutrients from other parts of the plant. A little judicious trimming not only keeps your plants looking good, it also encourages them to produce batches of fresh growth. More about this on the opposite page. A proper bath takes time, so if you have a lot of plants, do only a few per session.

### Pruning or pinching makes a plant grow bushier.

Leggy, elongated growth is a sure sign that this Green Emerald Philodendron has gotten out of hand and needs cutting back. Don't worry about hurting a plant by pruning or pinching; it'll actually relish the opportunity to send out fresh shoots, especially in spring or summer periods when it's most active.

For plants like the Green Emerald, trim just beyond a leaf node with a scissors or knife. Larger plants that you want to shape up will require some study. On many of your plants you can root the resulting cuttings in water and start new plants, as shown on pages 45 to 48.

Pinching growth buds offers a less drastic way to shape growth. But don't pinch single-stem plants such as a Dieffenbachia, Rubber Tree or dracaenas.

### What should you do about overgrown roots?

There comes a time when even the happiest of Deco Plants starts thinking about a new home. It'll tell you this by sending out numerous roots through the slots in its Planting Basket. When this happens, you have two alternatives to choose from.

The first is to give in to the plant's demands and repot it in the next larger size Plantset container, as explained on pages 47 and 48. Work carefully and you'll probably be able to pull all or most of the roots back through the slots as you remove the plant.

If you don't want to repot, trim off the excess root growth and the plant will maintain a size compatible with its present container. To minimize shock, remove only a third of the roots growing beyond the container at a time and wait a week between cuttings.

### For a really shaped look, train climbers to follow a trellis or other support system.

Some plants, such as ivies and some philodendrons, are born showoffs. Provide them with a framework of some sort and soon they'll be scrambling over it like a cage full of monkeys.

The framework might be as simple as a plastic trellis or a couple of thin bamboo stakes, as subtle as a network of fishline, or as imaginative as the coat hanger hoop that shapes this leafy "handle."

In shaping your plant's figure, bear in mind that new growth always heads for sunlight. This means you won't have much luck if the existing foliage receives good light but your support doesn't. Get new growth started by securing tendrils with kitchen ties. When the plant grabs hold, remove the ties.

# CHAPTER 3
# Stamp out pest problems

One plant party you *don't* want to play hostess for is the kind that's attended by any of a variety of different insects. These sociable little fellows love plants almost as much as people do—but to them your favorite green things are just so much salad.

With the Soilfree Deco Plantsystem you rarely need to worry about pests that do their dirty work belowground. Even the nicest plants, though, occasionally attract some unwanted guests.

The following pages introduce you to the pests you're most likely to encounter—their habits, likes and dislikes, and how to keep your plants healthy and free from trouble.

## Plant pests ...the big five

## Spider Mites

To a spider mite, the leaf of a medium-size houseplant must seem as vast as the state of California. These eight-legged critters—cousins of ordinary spiders and sometimes called red spiders—measure only about 1/50 of an inch long, so don't expect to get a good look at one without the help of a strong magnifying glass.

In good light, though, you can see colonies with your naked eye. Look at the undersides of leaves, especially along the veins and edges where mites like to congregate; a bronze or reddish hue means they're at work sucking away your plant's vital juices.

**Symptoms:** Whitish or yellowish speckled spots on the tops of leaves are your first clue that spider mites have arrived. Eventually, leaves take on a bronze or yellow look and may die or drop off. Silky webbing, like the frail strands at left, means your plant has a bad case.

**Life cycle:** Spider mites begin life as eggs and live for about a month. During that time, the number of eggs one of these characters can lay depends largely upon temperature. At 60 degrees, one female will produce only about 20 eggs—not a big family in the mite world. Increase the temperature to 80 degrees and her tribe could potentially reach 13 million! The eggs like it hot, too. At 80 degrees, they'll hatch in about five days—at 60 degrees, almost 15 days. Seven days is typical. This explains why spider mites seem to go wild in warm locations or during those first hot days of spring or summer. They thrive in dry environments, too.

As populations explode, mite-gration begins. Young females glide on their silky threads to other leaves—or ride air currents, clothes, or your hands to other plants. Some even set out on foot.

**Susceptible plants:** Dracaenas, Dumb Cane, palms, scheffeleras, aralias, Zebra and Prayer Plants, Crotons, philodendrons, Peace Lilies and most ivies.

**Controls:** Since cooler temperatures and higher humidity levels greatly inhibit mites, try to provide these conditions for susceptible plants.

Periodically check all plants for spider mites, as explained above. Be especially vigilant during warm periods. And if you happen to take your plant outdoors, check it carefully before you bring it in. Isolate it from your other plants for a week or two, then check again. Spider mites abound in outside vegetation.

If you spot evidence of mites, isolate the plant immediately and bathe it weekly with mildly soapy water. Be sure to wash away any webbing and give the undersides of leaves a good scrubbing. This will remove all or most of the adults, but it won't affect the eggs. To get these, you have to wait a week until they hatch, then wash again. Repeat once more a week later.

**Insecticides:** You can also spray with a miticide containing tetradifon or dicofol. Again, repeat weekly for three weeks or more to kill off newly hatched mites.

It's not hard to recognize mealybugs. They look like many-legged blobs—about the size of a baby's fingernail—that have been rolled in flour. You'll see them creeping slowly along stems and the undersides of leaves, and find their eggs suspended in cottony sacks (see Hoya at right). Some also attack roots.

Mealybugs feed by piercing plant surfaces with mouths that work like hypodermic needles. As they suck out sap, they also excrete a sticky substance which coats the foliage. Called "honeydew," this excretion first looks like honey, but soon turns a moldy black. The sticky coating makes it difficult for the plant to breathe, and may also attract ants.

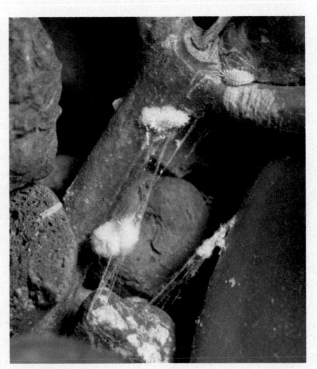

**Symptoms:** Usually you can see the insects themselves, their eggs, and the honeydew. Like most pests, mealybugs don't like light, so look for them on the undersides of leaves and stems. Root-feeding mealybugs cause plants to grow slowly and wilt between feedings. If you think a plant has them, remove some Living Stones and you may see blobs at work just below the surface.

**Life cycle:** Mealybugs are on the move most of their lives, and since they live for six weeks to two months, just one can cover a lot of plant surfaces. Females mature, lay their eggs, then die. The eggs hatch in five to ten days, or wait longer until conditions are more to their liking. All this means that if just one mealybug— or one egg sack—survives your treatment, the insects will continue to feed and breed.

*Mealy Bugs*

**Susceptible plants:** African Violets seem especially attractive to mealybugs, but you can also find them on the Chinese Evergreen, Wax or Hoya Plants, boxwood, Jade Plant, Devil's Ivy, Marble Queen, Prayer Plant, aralias and other species.

**Controls:** On hairy-leaved or spiny plants, dab each bug with a cotton swab that's been dipped in rubbing alcohol, then rinse the leaves in lukewarm, chemical-free water. With smooth-leaved plants, wash with a solution of two teaspoons of mild dish detergent to a gallon of water. Expect the mealybugs to resist this treatment—they're protected by a waterproof wax. Isolate the plant in case you've missed any bugs or eggs, and check again in a week or so. You'll probably need to wash a second and maybe a third time as well. If a plant has just a few root-feeding mealybugs, you may be able to get rid of them with alcohol. If not, resign yourself to propagating a new one by taking a cutting and discarding the infested plant.

**Insecticides:** For severe infestations, spray with malathion or Diazinon—or an aerosol formulated for mealybugs. Check the manufacturer's label first, though. This chemical can be toxic to certain plant species. To minimize any possible damage, apply pesticides during cool hours of the day and let them dry in a ventilated space. Spray again after 7 and 14 days.

*Scale*

Scale insects resemble tiny turtles . . . but they're even lazier. Like turtles, scale have hard shells—1/16 to 1/8 inch in diameter, usually brown or green in color. Unlike turtles, scale don't move around after they mature; instead, they afix themselves to a plant leaf or stem and feed off its juices.

You can easily spot wart-like adults lined up along a leaf vein, as shown at left, or attached barnacle-fashion to stems. Baby scale are a different matter. Shell-less and invisible to the naked eye, they crawl about seeking fresh foliage to get their teeth into.

**Symptoms:** Scale can sometimes be mistaken for mealybugs. Look closely, though, and you'll see a shell instead of the mealybug's waxy white covering. Many scale shells are simply round or oval domes. Others look like miniature oyster shells. Scratch one with your fingernail or the blade of a knife and it'll pop free.

Also like mealybugs, most scale excrete droplets of a sweetish, sticky "honeydew" that gives foliage a shiny look. This gooey stuff attracts black mold, and sometimes ants as well.

**Life cycle:** When babies—called crawlers—leave home they have legs and antennae to help them in their wanderings. Since they can travel for as long as two days without feeding, they're hardy enough to drop off one plant and seek out another.

Once a crawler finds a likely homestead, it sinks its mouth into the leaf or stem, then tucks its legs under its body and settles down. Eventually the legs and antennae disappear and a shell begins to form. This continues to enlarge, providing protection for new generations of scale born underneath. Females produce three to seven broods in a year's time.

**Susceptible plants:** Scale are especially fond of palms and ivy, but also thrive on scheffleras, boxwood, Jade Plants, aralias, Chinese Evergreens, dracaenas, philodendrons, Peace Lilies and Weeping Figs.

**Controls:** High humidity levels make it difficult for scale insects to make headway. In dry winter months you might want to consider running a humidifier near susceptible plants.

For light infestations, dislodge scale with a soft toothbrush or wet cloth—or dab with denatured alcohol, just as you would for mealybugs. Once you've popped off a shell, make sure you also get the eggs underneath. Wash with soapy water and quarantine the plant for several weeks. You may have to repeat the treatment several times. Discard heavily infested plants or they'll infect healthy ones.

**Insecticides:** Chemical sprays containing malathion, Diazinon and other insecticides easily knock out crawlers, but they can't penetrate the adults' shells. Get rid of the mature ones first, as explained above, then spray to prevent a new outbreak. Check for scale and spray again in a week to ten days.

Most plant pests are shy creatures who prefer to lurk in dim crannies where they can't be easily detected. Not aphids. These bold, gregarious insects work right out in the open. On infested plants you can find entire colonies of them cavorting on new growth, at the base of buds, and on the undersides of leaves.

Usually less than 1/8 inch long, commonly greenish white or black, aphids have soft, pear-shaped bodies, long legs and antennae. Most are wingless, but winged versions appear when a colony gets too crowded and decides to migrate to another plant.

**Symptoms:** Aphid feeding causes poor growth, stunted plants or curled and distorted leaves. Developing aphids shed white skins. A pile of them on upper leaf surfaces may be your first sign that these destructive insects have arrived.

In the process of sucking out plant juices, aphids—like mealybugs and scale—excrete a sweetish, sticky "honeydew" that often turns a moldy black and may lure ants. Aphids also carry viral diseases to plants.

**Life cycle:** Females seem to like enormous families. A single aphid typically gives birth to between 60 and 100 young ones every day—for a period of 20 to 30 days. And each of her daughters is able to reproduce within seven to 10 days. Their high birth rate, coupled with aphids' ability to sprout wings and migrate, means you should take action as soon as you spot them. Immediately isolate the infested plant, or any other plants in your house might be settled by a new colony.

# Aphids

**Susceptible plants:** Scheffleras, aralias, Hoya and Zebra Plants are particularly prone to aphids—but once they get started, these nuisances aren't fussy.

**Controls:** Fortunately, new aphid populations aren't difficult to get rid of. Wash the foliage in soapy water—rinsing with a sink sprayer if possible—and they'll usually leave in a hurry. Don't be deceived, though; new generations may crop up, so check and treat again after seven days. For best results, repeat a third time. If a plant has only a few aphids, you may be able to control them by dabbing with a cotton swab soaked in rubbing alcohol.

**Insecticides:** Use Diazinon or an aerosol pest killer that lists both aphids and houseplants on its label—and follow the directions carefully. Some pesticides can't be sprayed indoors (you'll have to take the plant outside), and none should be applied when children, pets or food are in the vicinity. To be really safe, let sprayed plants dry in the garage.

Realize, too, that it'll take three sprayings, at seven-day intervals, to knock out aphids. If the insecticide you're using doesn't seem as effective as it used to be, switch to one based upon a different chemical. Like many pests, aphids sometimes develop immunities to a poison; spraying with another usually catches them off guard.

## White Flies

If brushing against a plant seems to set off a small snowstorm, don't suspect dandruff—your plant probably has a case of white flies. These tiny, mothlike insects take flight every time their home is moved, making them a nuisance to people and pets, as well as a destroyer of plant foliage.

White flies measure about 1/16 inch long, have a powdery stuff on their bodies and sport wedge-shaped wings. At rest, the flies fold their wings into a roof over their bodies, which makes them seem all the more like newfallen snowflakes.

**Symptoms:** White flies damage plants in much the same ways that aphids do—sucking juices from leaves and secreting large quantities of sticky "honeydew." Glistening at first, the honeydew soon turns a moldy black. Infested leaves pale, turn yellow and die or drop off. Young flies resemble scale. Pale green to yellow-white, they're oval in outline and flat on top, and attach themselves to the undersides of new leaves.

**Life cycle:** White flies begin as small eggs, which may be covered with powdery materials. Then they go through several crawling and dormant stages. These pests typically start out at the top of a plant and work their way down. With eggs clinging to the lower surfaces of tender new growth, adolescents and adults feed off the leaves below. On the bottommost leaves of an infested plant you may find empty skins shed by the flies above. A mature female usually lays several hundred eggs during her month-long life-span.

**Susceptible plants:** Though not as big a threat to houseplants as spider mites, mealybugs, scale, and aphids, white flies like African Violets, Peace Lilies, ivies, palms, and scheffleras.

**Controls:** Washing foliage in a mildly soapy solution makes an excellent preventive. But if you've seen evidence of flies, washing may not be totally effective. It will get rid of eggs and crawlers—but the adults can simply take flight and return later, or migrate to another plant. Insecticides are best here.

**Insecticides:** Spray with a formulation that contains malathion, Diazinon, rotenone and pyrethrin. Take special care to get the undersides of all leaves. Repeat this treatment twice, at seven-day intervals, to kill off any new generations. And keep the plant in isolation for several weeks, until you're sure the flies are gone.

One problem with pesticides is that they sometimes poison the patient as well as the pest. Too strong a dose—or an insecticide that's not right for the plant—may partially or totally burn leaves, distort them or leave spots. Usually this happens with the oldest, most developed leaves. These may drop off, but new ones will form, and the plant generally recovers within a few weeks. To minimize troubles, always read the label on a spray before you use it, and follow the manufacturer's instructions to the letter.

Thrips aren't housebroken, which makes them messy but fairly easy to detect. If it weren't for their droppings—and the damage these tiny, shy insects do—you'd hardly know they were around. Adults are almost microscopic in size, with slender bodies that are tan-to-brown-to-black with yellow markings. Many have two sets of wings, which they use for quick getaways when you might be looking.

Thrips feed with rasp-like jaws, shredding plant tissues and sucking juices. Injured areas turn white.

**Symptoms:** Look for silver-colored streaks speckled with little dots of black excrement. Thrips attack flowers as well as leaves. On infested plants, foliage may blotch or drop off, and flowers may be streaked or distorted.

One quick way to check for thrips is to tap a leaf you think might be infested against a sheet of white paper. If you get specks that move, you've dislodged some thrips and had better attend to the relatives they left behind.

**Life cycle:** Females bury their eggs in plant tissue. These hatch within a week into wingless nymphs, which then feed on everything they can get their rasping teeth into. Thrips live two to three weeks.

**Susceptible plants:** Thrips enjoy a broad diet of plant species, including philodendron, aralias, Zebra and Wax or Hoya Plants, Arrowhead Vines, ivies, Yuccas and Rubber and Weeping Fig Trees.

**Controls:** As with most insects, thrips are very active during the summer months, especially July. Check for them often in hot weather and spray plants with water periodically to discourage new populations.

If you find thrips, two or three washings with a mild detergent solution (two teaspoons to a gallon of water), followed with lukewarm rinses, usually eliminates them. Space the baths a week apart so you can treat any eggs soon after they hatch. And you'll want to keep the plant in quarantine until you're sure it's pest-free.

**Insecticides:** Spray with a malathion-based formulation. Read the container's label first to be sure the spray you've selected is effective against thrips and safe for the plant you'll be using it on. As with washing, repeat the treatment weekly. Two or three doses will be needed to completely knock out the insects. Caution: Always keep pesticides in their original containers, and store them on high shelves or in cabinets where children can't get at them.

# ...and other pest problems

## Cyclamen Mites

## Thrips

Though related to the spider mites discussed on page 34, cyclamen mites lead different lives. First of all, you can't even see one of these minute spiders without a powerful microscope. They measure just 1/100 of an inch long, and many types have semitransparent bodies as well.

Secondly, unlike spider mites, cyclamens don't spin webs. Instead they simply crawl from leaf to leaf and plant to plant—or hitch rides on your hands or clothing. And because cyclamen mites like to hide out in protected spots—on tender young leaves, stem ends, buds and flowers—you probably won't even know they're around until their handiwork begins to show.

**Symptoms:** Leaves begin to twist, curl, turn brittle or blacken. New growth may be stunted. On ivies infested with cyclamen mites, you'll see stems that have small, gnarled leaves, or no leaves at all; on African Violets, small, twisted, hairy leaves that soon die.

**Life cycle:** Females live about a month and lay more than 100 tiny, oval, glossy-white eggs. Tucked into crevices of buds and leaves, these hatch in three to seven days into slow-crawling larvae. The entire life cycle runs four to six weeks.

Unlike spider mites, which proliferate fastest in hot, dry environments, cyclamen mites develop more rapidly at high humidity levels and cooler temperatures. Outbreaks often occur in the fall and spring.

**Susceptible plants:** Though especially partial to Zebra Plants, ivies and African Violets, cyclamen mites will also attack a wide variety of other houseplants.

**Controls:** First, trim away all badly damaged leaves, buds, and other injured parts. Next, lift out the container's liner and immerse the plant—liner and all—in water heated to 110 degrees. Keep it there for 15 minutes, making sure you maintain the water at exactly 110 degrees. Finally, reassemble the container and add Nutrient. Check the foliage in 7 to 10 days for new damage. You may need to repeat treatment.

While you're waiting to find out, keep infested plants isolated and think of them as being in a contagious condition. Wash your hands after handling them and take care not to brush against leaves where would-be travelers might be lurking.

**Insecticides:** Spray with dicofol or an aerosol formulated to fight cyclamen mites, taking special care to get at the places where they like to hide. You'll need to do it two or three times at 10-day intervals.

Broad mites have a lot in common with both spider and cyclamen mites. Like spider mites, they breed and spread most rapidly in hot, dry environments. And like cyclamen mites, the adults are much too small to be seen without a microscope—about 1/100 of an inch long—and they don't spin telltale webs.

Broad mites aren't quite as sneaky as cyclamen mites. They lay sizable eggs right out in the open. On infested plants you'll see conspicuous white dots lined up in neat rows along leaf surfaces. Spot these and you'd better take action right away; broad mites don't live long, but they move fast and can do a lot of damage.

**Symptoms:** Broad mites like to feed off the lower surfaces of young leaves, which prevents the leaf from expanding normally and causes it to pucker in a downward direction. New leaves may also thicken, turn brittle, and develop serrated margins. New buds may drop off, and eventually the entire plant may die.

**Life cycle:** Eggs hatch in just two to three days, then these minute spiders set out walking and cover surprisingly vast plant territories, feeding as they move. Typically, broad mites live only four to six days. They lay more eggs and hatch faster at temperatures between 70 and 80 degrees, which explains why they spread fastest from spring to early fall.

**Susceptible plants:** Broad mites are especially fond of Zebra Plants, most ivies, and some types of peperomia. Occasionally, they'll attack other plants as well.

**Controls:** Maintaining cooler temperatures does a lot to discourage these pests. As soon as you see any evidence of infestation, set the plant off by itself. Wash your hands after handling it. Don't risk contaminating other plants.

Exterminate broad mites as you would spider mites—by thoroughly bathing foliage with a mild detergent solution. Pay special attention to the undersides of leaves where adults and youngsters feed. Follow up with a second washing after a week and a third a week after that. Some eggs might survive the first and even the second treatment.

**Insecticides:** Spray three times, at weekly intervals, with a miticide containing malathion or dicofol. Be warned that mites are especially good at developing immunities to certain chemicals. If repeated doses of a malathion-based spray doesn't seem to do the job, try switching to one that has dicofol—or wash the plant as explained above.

## ...and other pest problems

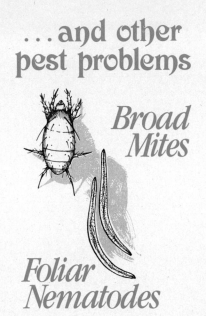

### Broad Mites

### Foliar Nematodes

Nematodes—microscopic creatures sometimes called eelworms or roundworms—generally live in soil and attack plants through their root systems. This means that most aren't a big threat to Deco Plants . . . a good thing, since about all you can do with infested plants is destroy them.

Occasionally, though, the foliar type will take up residence even in water-rooted plants. If that should happen at your house, you'll want to take action right away—before the problem turns into an epidemic and the nematodes spread to other Deco Plants in your home.

**Symptoms:** Don't plan on seeing foliar nematodes with the naked eye, however. They are microscopic in size, and only a laboratory can properly diagnose an infection. Foliar nematodes live inside plant cells, gradually eating at them from the inside out. Stems begin to swell, branching becomes irregular, and brown or black areas show up between leaf veins. Typically, these spots first appear on the undersides of bottommost leaves, then work through to the upper sides.

**Life cycle:** Nematodes begin as eggs and pass through four larval stages before they mature into adults. One reason they're so hard to eradicate is that second-stage larvae must feed before they develop any further. Waiting for their first meals, they'll outlast almost any chemical, and not begin growth until encountering a susceptible plant. Once they're aboard, though, foliar nematodes develop and multiply rapidly.

**Susceptible plants:** Red and Green Emerald Philodendrons and Abidjan Rubber Trees are the only Deco Plants that are especially vulnerable to foliar nematodes, but keep an eye out for them with almost any specimen transplanted from soil that might not have been sterilized. If a plant dies and you suspect—but aren't certain—nematodes were the culprits, check with a botanical or agricultural service in your region. Many have labs that will conduct a post-mortem.

**Controls:** As noted above, resign yourself to discarding any infested plant—container and all. It's best not to take the chance of reinfecting a new plant with an improperly sterilized container. Don't try to propagate it, either. If you choose to mist plants, don't let water splash from leaf to leaf. It can spread nematodes and other problems.

**Insecticides:** Don't put too much hope here, either. Vydate L, Mocap and Dasanit are sometimes effective. Your best bet is to buy a new healthy plant.

# PEST PROBLEMS . . . AND SOLUTIONS . . . AT A GLANCE

| INSECT | PROBLEM | SOLUTION |
|---|---|---|
| **Spider Mites** | First, leaf tops develop white or yellow spots. Later they take on a bronze look and may die or drop off. Advanced cases have silky webbing extending from leaf to leaf—especially in crevices. | Wash with a mild detergent solution (2 tsp./gal. of water). Or, spray with a miticide such as dicofol or tetradifon (1½ tsp./gal.). Repeat treatment every 7 days for 2 to 3 weeks. |
| **Mealybugs** | White, many-legged blobs and cottony egg sacks under leaves and stems; a sticky coating of honeydew that often attracts black mold and sometimes ants, too. | Dab each bug with a swab moistened in denatured alcohol, or wash with a mild detergent solution; spray with malathion (1½ tsp./gal.) or Diazinon (2 tsp./gal.). |
| **Scale** | Shell-like creatures—1/16 to 1/8 inch in diameter—attach to stems or the tops of leaves; like mealybugs, scales also excrete honeydew that soon turns black MAY be brown or green in color. | Dislodge them with a soft toothbrush, or dab with a swab soaked in rubbing alcohol. Wash with soapy water. Or, spray with malathion (1½ tsp./gal.) or Diazinon (2 tsp./gal.). |
| **Aphids** | Usually you can see aphids hopping about on leaf surfaces. They cause poor growth, stunted plants or distorted leaves, which may also be coated with honeydew. | Wash with mild detergent solution or spray with Diazinon (2 tsp./gal.). Repeat again after a week—and yet again a week after that—to kill off new generations. |
| **White Flies** | Small, white, mothlike insects that flutter from leaves when you brush against them. Infested leaves turn yellow and die; white flies also excrete honeydew. | Spray with a malathion (1½ tsp./gal.), Diazinon (2 tsp./gal.), or pyrethrin formulation at weekly intervals for 2 or 3 weeks. Don't miss undersides of leaves. |
| **Thrips** | White or silvery streaks dotted with black excrement. Leaves may blotch or drop off. Buds or flowers may be streaked or distorted as well the plant foliage. | Wash with a mild detergent solution or spray with malathion (2 tsp./gal.). Repeat every 7 days for 2 more weeks to eliminate any eggs that escaped treatments. |
| **Cyclamen Mites** | Leaves twist, curl, turn brittle or blacken. New growth may be stunted, with gnarled leaves or none at all. Ivies and African Violets are especially prone. | Put plant and liner in water heated to precisely 110 degrees for 15 minutes. Or spray with dicofol (1½ tsp./gal.) two or three times at 10-day intervals. |
| **Broad Mites** | Rows of white eggs lined up along leaf surfaces. Leaves pucker in a downward direction. They may also thicken, turn brittle, and develop serrated margins. | Bathe leaves in a mild dish detergent solution, or spray with malathion (2 tsp./gal.) or dicofol (1½ tsp./gal.). Repeat either treatment after 7 and 14 days. |
| **Foliar Nematodes** | Microscopic in size, they live inside plant cells. Stems begin to swell, branching becomes irregular, and brown or black areas show up between leaf veins. Spots usually first appear on undersides of bottommost leaves. | If you suspect foliar nematodes, have a botanical center or laboratory check for sure. Resign yourself to discarding any infested plant. Vydate L, Mocap and Dasanit are sometimes used. Best bet is to start over with a healthy new plant. |

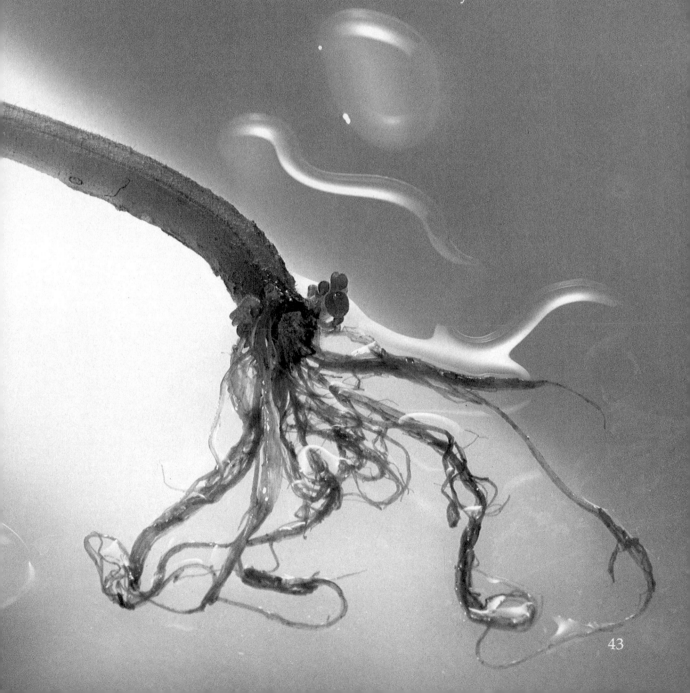

# CHAPTER 4

# Give your plants a fresh start

Think of the Garden of Eden and you'll get an understanding of how most houseplants reproduce—they spring from each other, like Eve from Adam. On a large number of plants, you simply cut off part of a plant you'd like to see more of, stick it in a glass of water—and wait.

Soon the cutting sends forth its own tiny roots and fresh growth, like those at the base of the African Violet leaf shown here. It's just about ready to wrap its newly grown roots around the Living Stones in a Plantset container—and after that the Soilfree Deco Plantsystem takes over.

43

# Take a leaf cutting

Of all the ways to get a new plant going, rooting a leaf cutting is one of the easiest. You simply snip off a leaf or leaves—depending on how many plantlets you want—insert it in water, and wait for roots to develop. This technique works best with the African Violet, Peperomia, Hoya, Jade and Snake Plant.

**Select a mature, healthy leaf, and cut** the leaf's stem (petiole) at its base, near a main stem. Don't try to pull leaf from plant or sever petiole with your fingernail. Instead, use a sharp knife, razor blade, or shears you know will make a clean cut. Steady the leaf with one hand to assure that you don't loosen the plant roots.

Next, trim the leaf's stem at an angle to a length of one half to one inch. For most plants, such as the African Violet shown here, you're now ready for *step 2*. If you're making a leaf cutting of a Snake Plant, however, you also need to cut the leaf itself into three-inch-long segments.

(Snake plants propagated in this way lose their characteristic yellow stripes; to retain these markings, try root division, as explained on pages 49 and 72.)

**Fill a drinking glass with water,** and add a tablespoon of charcoal to keep it fresh. Then stretch a piece of aluminum foil or wax paper over the top and secure it with a rubber band. Now, poke small holes (just big enough for stem ends) in the covering and insert the cuttings. Don't make the holes too big or the leaves will fall out.

If you've cut up a Snake Plant leaf, as explained in *step 1*, be sure you insert the sections in their upright positions; roots won't form it the leaves are upside-down. Immerse half of each segment.

You'll need an additional hole in the center so you can add water as needed, and a couple of smaller holes to help aerate the water. In this environment, your cutting will develop the proper root system.

**Set the glass on a windowsill**—but not in direct sun. Before long you'll see new growth—first roots, then some fledgling leaves or new shoots—sprouting from the cut end. Exactly how long the rooting process will take depends upon the plant species—six weeks is typical. You'll know a cutting is ready for potting in a Deco container when roots are two to three inches long and new growth has begun.

Handle cuttings gingerly when you remove them from the glass. Like all babies, young water roots are tender, delicate things. Tear the foil or paper so rooted cuttings can be removed easily.

To learn about establishing each of your new plantlets in its very own Soilfree Deco Plantsystem environment, turn to page 47.

To root most houseplants you need more than a single leaf. The Arrowhead Vine, Chinese Evergreen, Dracaena, Ivy and Philodendron are just a few of the species that propagate more readily from tip or stem cuttings. The photographs below illustrate how to go about taking both types of cuttings from a Golden Pothos.

# Take a tip or stem cutting

**For a tip cutting,** remove the final four to six inches of a vine, as shown here. Make the cut below a leaf node. As with leaf cuttings, select mature, healthy growth, do the job with a sharp knife or shears, and firmly hold the portion being trimmed to prevent accidentally damaging the rest of the plant.

Don't worry about hurting your plant when you cut. Plants don't need anesthetics, and they'll send out new shoots wherever you prune. Try to propagate in the spring, when new growth is just getting started. This gives the cutting an opportunity to get well established before autumn.

Each tip cutting should include three or four leaf nodes. Trim off any leaves that will be beneath the water's surface. Otherwise, rot could set in.

*1*

**For a stem cutting,** you amputate only a single leaf and a portion of the stem it's attached to. The stem cutting should measure about 1½ inches long—1" of stem below the leaf, ½" above the leaf. Slice the stem at an angle. Only the stem portion should be inserted in water—just covering the leaf node.

This view also gives you a better look at our *tip* cutting, laying beside the pot. Note the small projection at the cut-off end. Roots develop quickly and well here, as shown below.

Ideally, all cuttings—whether leaf, tip or stem—should be put into water right away. If you can't do this, dampen them, place in a plastic bag, and keep in a cool place away from sunlight. They'll stay fresh for a few days.

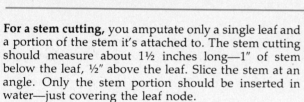

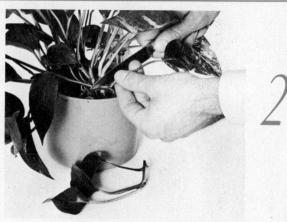

*2*

**Root stem and tip cuttings,** just as you would leaves—in a glass of water covered with aluminum foil or wax paper. A tablespoon of charcoal purifies the water and keeps odors from developing.

In a couple weeks, the cutting will send out roots like these. Note, too, that tiny shoots are beginning to rise from the stem portion at right. Don't be in a hurry to pot cuttings, though. This one isn't ready yet. Wait until the plantlet develops a more extensive network of roots, like the ones shown on the opposite and following pages.

To propagate a large number of cuttings, lay an inch or two of small, clean gravel in a tray, add water to just below the pebbles' surface, then stick the cuttings into the pebbles. *continued*

*3*

Now our rooted cutting (opposite page) is ready to be installed in a Deco container. The steps illustrated here and on the following page show how to do it. Follow the same procedures for repotting a mature Deco Plant that's outgrown its container—or for transplanting from soil to the Soilfree Deco Plantsystem.

# How to pot a rooted cutting...or repot a plant

**Begin by thoroughly rinsing the Living Stones** in lukewarm tap water. This removes any dust particles that may be adhering to them. Do the job in a colander or a kitchen straining basket.

If you're repotting from soil, invert the pot while cupping the top of the pot in your hand and gently tap the sides of the pot to remove plant and soil. It should drop neatly into your hand.

Carefully remove excess soil from around the plant and hold the root portion covered with soil under vigorously running lukewarm water. Be sure you flush away every trace of earth. A kitchen sink sprayer may help. Particles you miss could lead to root rot once the plant is transplanted. Handle the root system gently to avoid excessive breakage.

**Fill about one third of the Planting Basket with Living Stones.** The top of the stones should be about even with the slits in the sides of the basket.

Next, tear open the covering on your rooting glass and gently remove the cutting. If you're repotting from another Deco container, carefully tip the basket and let the root system slide out, stones and all, into your cupped hand. Try to disturb these stones—and the roots wrapped around them—as little as possible. Roots that have grown through the slits in the Planting Basket may have to be trimmed away, as explained on page 31, if the plant cannot be easily removed. And, if you'll be using a freestanding moisture level indicator, place it flush with the bottom of the container, then add one third of the stones.

**Place the plant in the container** and spread out its roots overtop the Living Stones. Don't just stick the roots in one spot or the resulting root mass will rot. Use your fingers to carefully separate and distribute them evenly while you support the plant with your other hand.

Don't bury the roots at this point, either. They should never be lower than two-thirds of the basket's depth. The bottom third serves as a reservoir for the Nutrient Solution you'll be adding. Roots forced into this area against their will could get root rot. Let plant roots seek their own moisture level. When properly transplanted, you needn't worry about drowning your plant's roots; a Deco Plant's roots will seek—and find—the level it likes best. *continued*

47

# How to pot a rooted cutting...or repot a plant *Continued*

*4*

**Now sprinkle more Living Stones** around the rooted cutting, filling the container to the top. If you're potting several plants in the same container for a bushier look, space them out and fill between them with stones before topping up.

As you handle the stones, you'll notice how lightweight and fuzzy-textured they feel. Their weight and smooth surfaces protect delicate root systems from bruises when the container is moved. The texture helps water cling as it climbs up between stones.

Tested throughout Europe and imported from Germany, Living Stones promote more capillary action than nearly any other material. They're also sterile and inert—so they don't affect the Plantsystem's chemical balance one way or another.

*5*

**Gently tap sides of container** so the stones can settle in. This fills in air pockets and gives the roots more surface to grip. Then, carefully tug on the plant, lifting it to its natural growing line at the stem's base. This brings the roots into a more vertical position in the Living Stones—the way they'll ultimately grow.

If you can see roots on top of the stones after you have finished, you've lifted the plant too high or have not properly placed the roots in the beginning. Dump out the Living Stones and start over again. If no roots are visible, but the stones don't quite cover the stem's base, simply add more.

Now your newly potted Deco Plant is ready for its first good drink. You have a choice of refreshments to serve, however, so don't start pouring yet.

*6*

**Add Nutrient Solution—or just tepid water.** Which you select depends upon whether you have potted a rooted cutting or have transplanted from soil. Cuttings are ready for Nutrient as soon as they're potted. In fact, they can begin their Nutrient Solution diets two or three weeks beforehand—as soon as each has a firm set of roots—while they are still in their rooting glass.

Transplants, however, should drink only water for the first four weeks after potting. This gives them a chance to acclimate themselves to the Soilfree Deco Plantsystem and develop water roots.

Also, any newly potted Deco Plant—whether it began life as a cutting or in soil—should get reduced light for its first two weeks. If yours begins to wilt, mist it two or three times daily—or as often as needed.

As you may have already guessed, most plants are delighted to present you with offspring. Cut one almost anywhere, provide some moisture, and soon it'll be sending out a brand new root system, ready for potting. Here are three more techniques you can use to help your Deco Plants become proud parents.

# Other ways to start new plants

**Air-layering** offers a way to revitalize large plants with thick, woody stems—such as the Dracaenas, Dieffenbachia, Schefflera, Fig Tree and Philodendron—that have grown tall and sparse.

Start by making an incision in the trunk about two to three inches below its bottommost leaves. Insert a wood matchstick to hold open the cut, then wrap a baseball-sized clump of moist sphagnum moss around it. Cover this with plastic wrap secured by kitchen ties, as shown.

Keep the moss damp for several weeks or months, until roots form and fill the plastic. Now cut off the stem below the roots, rinse away every trace of the moss, and pot as explained on pages 47 and 48. Also, new shoots should sprout from the cut-off stem.

*Photograph: William Hopkins*

1

**Offsets** sometimes pop up right beside a mature plant, such as this Dieffenbachia, providing a ready-made plantlet that's yours for the potting.

To separate it from Mom, remove Living Stones until you can see where the two are connected, then sever them with a sharp knife. Take as many roots with the offset as possible—but be sure you leave the mother with enough to survive on.

If the offset's roots are well-developed, you can pot it right away in a Deco container. If not, immerse them in water, as you would a stem cutting, and wait for the roots to expand before potting.

Other plants that lend themselves to propagating in this way include the Dracaena, Palm, Peperomia and African Violet.

2

**Root division** also works with African Violets—and almost any other plant that grows in clumps from separate stems. You simply separate it into two or more sections, then pot each individually.

To divide roots, you'll have to remove the entire plant from the Living Stones and study how its roots are growing. In some cases they'll be intertwined and you can just pull them apart. Others may build on each other to form one large root ball. With these, it's best to cleanly slice through the roots rather than risk tearing them apart and damaging the plants.

Early spring, when plants are just beginning to start new growth, is the best time to divide roots. Whenever a divisible plant has outgrown its pot, consider whether you want to move up to a bigger one or divide.

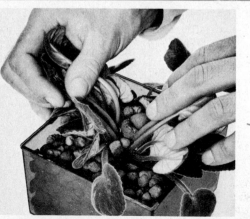

3

49

# CHAPTER 5

# 53 Favorite houseplants and how to grow them

One of the most lovable things about plants is that each is unique and has its own personality. Some plants started on the floors of dense jungles and are distinctly shady characters. Others evolved in mountain fields and are happiest in full sun. Some like it hot. Others cool. And some don't seem to care.

Success with any plant begins with making it feel at home. That means finding the place in your home which comes closest to the plant's original environment. Later, as a new plant settles in, the Deco Plantsystem automatically provides the water and food it needs. But you'll still want to know how to shape its growth, who its enemies are, and—if you and the plant hit it off—how you can get some little ones going.

The pictorial guide that follows shows and tells all this and more about each of the 53 Deco Plants America loves best. Consult these pages whenever you have a question about those you already own, or want to get off to a good start with any others you might be tempted to try.

## Chinese Evergreen
*Aglaonema modestum*

The first of a sizable family to be brought to the West from southern China, Borneo, and Malaysia, Chinese Evergreen grows to a height of two or three feet, with tapered leaves that dip at their tips. Its monochromatic foliage makes an excellent background for more colorful or variegated plants.

*Light:* Chinese Evergreen thrives in low to high indirect light. Full sun will burn the leaves.
*Temperature range:* 65 to 85 degrees.
*Special notes:* This one prefers a moist atmosphere but can survive under almost any humidity conditions. Watch out for mealybugs, scale and virus infection.

## Marble Queen
*Scindapsus aureus 'Marble Queen'*

The Marble Queen reigns over a family known as "Devil's Ivy," which is sometimes mistaken for philodendron. Train her to climb and she'll reach a height of six feet—or let her green-and-white leaves trail from a hanging basket.
*Light:* Medium to high, please; a north- or east-facing window is just fine for her majesty.
*Temperature range:* 55 to 85 degrees.
*Special notes:* Leaves darken and lose their markings as they age. Mealybugs or red spider mites are common problem insects. (If your plant has these pests, see pages 34 and 35.)

## Sweetheart Ivy
*Hedera helix 'Sweetheart'*

Heart-shaped leaves on this type of English Ivy have inspired countless romantic legends. One has it that if Sweetheart Ivy grows on a maiden's grave, she died of love.

You'll love Sweetheart's versatility. Train climbers on stakes or a trellis, let the vines trail from a hanging pot, or cut them back for a dense, compact mass.
*Light:* All English Ivies do well in medium to high filtered light, such as from a north or cool eastern exposure.
*Temperature range:* 55 to 80 degrees, cooler in winter months.
*Special needs:* Subject to scale and cyclamen mites. To test for mites, hold a sheet of white paper underneath leaves, tap the vines sharply, then look for tiny specks crawling on the paper.

**Chinese Evergreen**
*Aglaonema modestum*

**Marble Queen**
*Scindapsus aureus
'Marble Queen'*

**Sweetheart Ivy**
*Hedera helix 'Sweetheart'*

### African Violet
*Saintpaulia ionantha*

Not really violets at all (though they do come from the mountains of East Africa), African Violets have earned their immense popularity by blooming freely throughout the year. Be warned that once you've invited one to your windowsill, you'll soon want more.

*Light:* African Violets won't bloom in a room with low light intensity. If you don't get a distinct shadow cast on white paper where the plant sits, it's not getting enough light. East sun is best, except during the summer when you might want to try a cooler northern exposure or filter light through sheer curtains.

*Temperature range:* 65 to 85 degrees. Avoid sudden temperature changes, and move the plants away from windows on cool evenings.

*Special notes:* African Violets thrive under slightly dry conditions. Keep water off leaves and flowers, or they'll scorch in sunlight. And when you add Nutrient Solution, make sure it's lukewarm—never cooler than room temperature.

You can force-bloom African Violets with fluorescent grow-lights timed to turn off after 12 to 14 hours exposure. Set plants so the tops of their leaves are only about four inches from the lights. When buds start to open, move the plants to windowsill.

New plants propagate easily from leaf cuttings. To learn how to grow new plants, see page 44.

### Norfolk Island Pine
*Araucaria heterophylla*

This sturdy evergreen hails from a small island off the coast of Australia, where some ancient specimens have reached heights of 150 feet or more. Indoors, Norfolk Island Pine grows slowly—three to six inches a year—and tops off at somewhere between two and six feet. Its boughs radiate in tiers like spokes on a wheel. Deck them with ornaments at Christmas time.

*Light:* Avoid direct sun. Norfolk Island Pine likes medium to high indirect or diffused light. Too low an intensity will cause it to grow wider at the top.

*Temperature range:* 55 to 85 degrees.

*Special notes:* If needles on lower branches start to turn brown, cut them off flush with the trunk. If your plant becomes straggly, cut off the top 12 to 15 inches and root it as described on pages 45 to 48. Discard the parent plant. You can also root individual branches, but you'll get an irregular curved shape rather than the upright symmetrical form most people prefer.

**Norfolk Island Pine**
*Araucaria heterophylla*

**African Violet**
*Saintpaulia ionantha*

## Arrowhead Vine or
## Variegated Nephthytis
*Syngonium podophyllum 'Roxanne'*

In her native Mexico, Roxanne (sometimes called Variegated Nephthytis) is a sociable climber who loves to wrap herself around tree trunks in search of sunlight. You can train her enthusiasm for climbing indoors, too, although this relative of the philodendron takes awhile to mature into a vining plant.

Multi-tone, arrow-shaped leaves, ranging in size up to five inches, give *Syngonium* its nickname. Its long, willowy stems can reach a height of several feet.

*Light:* Roxanne does best in medium to high intensities.

*Temperature range:* 60 to 85 degrees.

*Special notes:* Keep size within bounds by pinching back new shoots. This one is especially easy to propagate with stem cuttings; when an older plant gets unsightly, cut the parent back radically and use the cuttings for new plants. Arrowhead Vine is subject to thrips and bacterial leafspot.

## Holly Ivy
*Hedera helix 'Holly'*

For a festive atmosphere all year long, deck your halls—or any other room for that matter—with pots of Holly. She'll climb almost anything her aerial roots can get a grip on, or let her trail freely from a hanging container.

Begin Holly's training while she's still young. Pinch off the ends of new shoots frequently, and you'll get lots of new lateral growth. These will happily climb a support—such as a wire coat hanger shaped into a hoop (see page 31) for a topiary effect.

*Light:* Medium to high intensities give the leaves a healthy, dark green sheen.

*Temperature range:* Like most ivies, Holly likes her environment a bit on the cool side—55 to 80 degrees.

*Special notes:* Start new vines by taking six- to eight-inch cuttings of medium-mature growth. Beware of cyclamen mites and scale.

## Heart-leaf Philodendron
*Philodendron scandens oxycardium*

It was Captain William Bligh—the very same man the crew of HMS *Bounty* mutinied against—who first brought the Heart-leaf Philodendron from the West Indies to En-gland. Today, it's one of the most popular of all houseplants—and with good reason. It'll climb, trail or stand on its own, and you can grow one almost anywhere but in direct sunlight or in a windowless closet. If you haven't had much luck with plants in the past, take a Heart-leaf to your heart.

*Light:* Anywhere from low to high intensities. The brighter the light, the bigger its leaves will grow.

*Special notes:* It's easy to root stem tip cuttings. To learn how, see pages 45 and 46. Provide support if you want your plant to climb. Thrips can be a problem. For information about other philodendron species, turn to pages 57 and 59.

## Janet Craig Dracaena
*Dracaena deremensis 'Janet Craig'*

Stiff, dark, corrugated leaves make it easy to distinguish Janet from her many brothers and sisters (see pages 57, 61, 66, 69 and 70). She'll grow tall—as high as 10 feet if you let her—so although you may want to start Janet on a tabletop, she'll eventually stand on the floor.

Mature specimens develop cane-like stalks. Don't be afraid to prune these if the plant gets leggy. Just saw off a cane at about four to six inches above the top of the pot. New sprouts will spring from the

**Arrowhead Vine**
*Syngonium podophyllum 'Roxanne'*

**Holly Ivy**
*Hedera helix 'Holly'*

**Heart-leaf Philodendron**
*Philodendron scandens oxycardium*

stump and provide a much bushier appearance.

*Light:* Medium to high, but no direct sun.

*Temperature range:* Maintain temperatures 60 to 85 degrees.

*Special notes:* Fluoride in the water can cause tip burning. If that's the case in your community (see page 26), use only pure, rain water. Don't worry about occasional brown spots; just snip them off. Sponge the leaves every so often with a damp cloth or mild soap solution. Check for scale and red spider mites.

## Parlor Palm
*Chamaedorea elegans 'Bella'*

Looking for an exotic, graceful floor plant that can add tropical elegance to just about any setting? Pick a palm. This one, which hails from Mexico, received its common name because of its popularity during Victorian times.

Parlor Palms still make sense today. They grow slowly, and top off at just three to four feet—as contrasted with other types, which sprout like weeds and can get out of hand in a short time.

*Light:* Medium to high, but keep away from direct sun.

*Temperature range:* 55 to 85 degrees.

*Special note:* Occasionally these sprout reddish-orange flowers, especially if you've summered one in a sheltered spot outdoors. Subject to red spider mites and scale. Palms will sprout slowly from seeds, but don't try to propagate them.

**Parlor Palm**
*Chamaedorea elegans 'Bella'*

**Janet Craig Dracaena**
*Dracaena deremensis 'Janet Craig'*

55

### Hawaiian Schefflera
*Brassaia arboricola*

Though not quite as much fun as an expense-paid trip to Honolulu, this glossy-leafed beauty offers a way to bring some of our 50th state's luxuriant foliage to any home setting. Most scheffleras grow tall—up to six feet—and because a flourishing one keeps sending up new branches, some tend to bush out as well. If yours gets top heavy and drops its lower leaves, you can start a new plant by air-layering the top, as explained on page 49.

Their size and verdant greenery mean scheffleras can either stand alone—at the end of a sofa, for example—or tower over a grouping of smaller plants. Don't, however, locate one where it might be easily bumped or brushed; the stems are brittle and snap off easily.

*Light:* Provide medium- to high-intensity illumination, but not direct sunlight.

*Temperature range:* 55 to 85 degrees.

*Special notes:* To maintain the leaves' attractive sheen, dust them regularly and clean periodically with a soft, damp cloth. Dull spots that resist the cloth usually can be buffed up by rubbing between your thumb and index finger. Keep an eye out for scale, spider mites and aphids—they like sch$f$fleras.

### Red-veined Prayer Plant
*Maranta leuconeura erythroneura*

Wait for nightfall, watch the *Maranta*'s exotic leaves fold upward—like hands pressed together palm to palm—and you'll see how this intriguing, colorful plant got its nickname. (Actually, it does this to conserve moisture.)

When you look for a place to put your Prayer Plant, think hard about the floor of a steamy jungle in Brazil. That's where *Marantas* come from, and a humid atmosphere makes them feel right at home.

Prayer Plants grow to a height of six or eight inches. When old leaves turn brown, especially in the winter, cut them off.

*Light:* This one tolerates a wide range of intensities, from low to high, but direct sunlight will wilt it almost immediately. A west or north window is ideal.

*Temperature range:* Avoid night temperatures below 55 degrees; days, the warmer the better—up to 85 degrees.

*Special notes:* To "wake up" a sleeping *Maranta*, place it under a lamp; the leaves will unfold in just a short time. Prayer Plants are prone to red spiders and mealybugs, and too much fluoride in the water can burn the tips of leaves.

**Hawaiian Schefflera**
*Brassaia arboricola*

**Red-veined Prayer Plant**
*Maranta leuconeura erythroneura*

## Gold Dust Dracaena
*Dracaena godseffiana*

Compared to other dracaenas, this little sparkler seems an impostor. Most of its cousins are tall, imposing plants, with elegant, striped foliage and a palmlike air. The Gold Dust stands just 18 to 24 inches high, and its leaves look as if they have the measles.

Sometimes called "Florida Beauty" (after the state where it was first cultivated), *D. godseffiana* makes an excellent accent among more somber greenery. And it shares the same iron-clad constitution common to all dracaenas; you needn't fuss overly much about growing conditions, the way you must with some other pattern-leafed plants.

*Light:* Locate away from direct sun, in medium to bright indirect or filtered light. The plant will survive low light situations, but its markings will fade.

*Temperature range:* 60 degrees minimum, 85 maximum. Keep away from drafts.

*Special notes:* Low humidity can occasionally bring spider mites. To ward them off, mist on sunny mornings. White cottony blobs mean mealybugs have attacked. Swab them off with cotton dipped in rubbing alcohol. If scale insects descend, wipe them away with a soft toothbrush dipped in sudsy water, or apply a chemical control. Avoid fluoridated water; it can cause tip burning.

You can start new dracaenas by air-layering or stem cutting. To learn about these techniques, see pages 44 to 49.

## Red Emerald Philodendron
*Philodendron x 'Red Emerald'*

Philodendrons might be considered the General Motors of the plant world. Though all share a few characteristics—leathery, usually glossy leaves, for instance—some bear no more resemblance to each other than a Chevy does to a Cadillac or a GMC truck.

Other philodendrons vary only slightly, like different models of the same make. The Red Emerald, for example, might be mistaken for the Green Emerald shown on page 59—except for the rosy tint on its stalks and undersides of its heart-shaped leaves.

Both are avid climbers and like to have a pole or trellis their aerial roots can cling to. To get vines started, gently tie the new growth to the post. Add additional ties to support the plant as it adds additional growth. If you prefer a more bushy, fuller plant, prune back the extra growth regularly. Removed cuttings can be rooted in water and eventually potted for adding to your Deco collection.

To learn about light, temperature ranges and other requirements, see page 59.

**Gold Dust Dracaena**
*Dracaena godseffiana*

**Red Emerald Philodendron**
*Philodendron x 'Red Emerald'*

57

**Silver King Evergreen**
*Aglaonema 'Silver King'*

**Green Emerald Philodendron**
*Philodendron x 'Green Emerald'*

**Danica Ivy**
*Cissus 'Ellen Danica'*

**Green Peperomia**
*Peperomia obtusifolia*

**Cupid Peperomia**
*Peperomia scandens 'Variegata'*

58

### Danica Ivy
*Cissus 'Ellen Danica'*

Though not really an ivy at all, Danica looks and behaves like one—and it's even easier to grow. Contrast its triple-clustered, brown-veined leaves with the "true" *Hedera* genus ivies shown on pages 63, 66 and 67.

One difference between *Hedera* and *Cissus* ivies can be traced to their origins. The former comes from northern Europe and Asia, while Danica is a native of the West Indies. This explains why it thrives at warmer temperatures than the so-called English ivies.

All make excellent climbers and trailers, though, and the more you pinch them back, the faster and fuller they seem to grow.
*Light:* Medium to high. Filtered, not direct sunlight.
*Temperature range:* Normal indoor temperatures—60 to 85 degrees—are just right. Drafts cause wilting.
*Special notes:* You can easily root Danica from six- to eight-inch stem cuttings (see pages 45 and 46). Red spider mites seem to like ivies almost as much as people do.

### Green Peperomia
*Peperomia obtusifolia*

Peperomias belong to a numerous and varied plant species that's sometimes called "semi-succulent."Genuine succulents, such as the cactus, store water for long periods of time, which helps them survive desert droughts. Peperomias hoard moisture, too, in their stems and chubby leaves. Don't expect one to go weeks without water. Most peperomias come from tropical regions of Venezuela, not a desert clime.

Green Peperomia has deep green, waxy, concave leaves. Its stalks grow upward for a time, then begin to lean over and trail as the plant reaches maturity.
*Light:* Supply medium to high light but no direct sun. A bright north or west window is good; filter intense sun elsewhere.
*Temperature range:* Maintain levels between 60 and 80 degrees.

*Special notes:* Don't be too quick to replenish your Green Peperomia's Nutrient when the indicator bottoms out. Since these plants hold moisture, they need to dry out between waterings; otherwise, stems will rot. If that happens, take stem or leaf cuttings and propagate them as explained on pages 44 and 45. Discard the ailing plant.

Be careful, too, that you don't confuse rot with ring spot, a virus infection. When this happens, growth is stunted and the leaves become marked with concentric rings. Throw out diseased plants; don't try to propagate them.

### Cupid Peperomia
*Peperomia scandens 'Variegata'*

Compare Cupid with the Green Peperomia next to it and you might think you're looking at different species. The truth is, Cupid is simply a hybridized version of the same plant.

Those colorful green and yellow leaves call for slightly different growing conditions, though—most notably brighter light if you want to maintain the markings.
*Light:* Medium to (preferably) high. Diffuse direct sunlight or the leaves will burn.
*Temperature range:* 60 to 80 degrees.
*Special notes:* As with Green Peperomia, it's easier to kill Cupid with kindness than with neglect. Let the plant dry out for a few days to prevent stem rot. Try to propagate the Cupid version and it'll come out with all-green leaves.

### Green Emerald Philodendron
*Philodendron x 'Green Emerald'*

This not-so-little gem looks exactly like the Red Emerald shown on page 57 except—you guessed it—its leaves are all-green, instead of red and green.
*Light:* As natives of rain forests, philodendrons can survive in almost any light level, but provide medium to high intensities for healthy growth. Hot, direct sun, however, will burn their leaves.
*Temperature range:* You'll get best results at 60 to 85 degrees. Don't

expose to drafts or abrupt temperature changes.
*Special notes:* Wash leaves monthly with a damp cloth. If they're really dirty, use mild dish detergent, but don't let any drip onto the Living Stones. To maintain the leathery sheen characteristic of philodendrons, buff the leaves with a soft, dry cloth.

Foliar nematodes, virus infections and scale can attack both Red and Green Emeralds. The green variety is also subject to red spiders and bacterial leafspot. To propagate philodendrons, take stem cuttings, as shown on page 45.

### Silver King Evergreen
*Aglaonema 'Silver King'*

Enthrone the king in a spot by himself, or let him preside over a court of lesser plants. Either way, his flashy foliage and sizable presence—two- to three-feet high at maturity—will bring a regal air to your home.

Native to China and other regions of Southeastern Asia, the Silver King is a hybrid of the Chinese Evergreen shown on page 52.

He's just as durable, too. Botanists believe, for instance, that those long, narrow, pointed leaves help him ride out the monsoon winds that regularly rip through the king's original habitat. (Broader-foliage plants would be stripped clean.) Monsoons probably aren't a big problem in your house, of course, but it's nice to know that the king is determined not to abdicate under practically any circumstances.

*Light: Aglaonema* can get by in just about any level from low to high—but under really shady conditions, the markings will fade. Avoid direct sun, too.
*Temperature range:* Silver King is quite happy in the warmth and low humidity of a home heated at 65 to 85 degrees.
*Special notes:* When stems grow too long, cut off their tops and re-root them. You can also propagate *Aglaonema* by root division. Pests include scale and mealybugs.

## Peace Lily
*Spathiphyllum 'Mauna Loa'*

For a touch of Easter throughout the year, keep Mauna Loa in bright light. Every so often she'll reward your kindness with white blossoms on long, slender stems.

This hybrid reaches a height of 24 to 30 inches, and its free-branching, feathery foliage makes it an excellent floor plant—either alone or as the main figure in a large grouping.
*Light:* Provide high light levels, but no direct sun. Mauna Loa can tolerate medium light, but won't flower in that situation.
*Temperature range:* 60 to 85 degrees is ideal.
*Special notes:* Don't be alarmed when leaves brown at the edges, then turn yellow; they've simply aged and should be cut off. Watch out, though, when only tips yellow. This usually means there's too much fluoride in the water. Mauna Loa's other enemies: red spider mites and scale.

## Croton Elaine
*Codiaeum 'Elaine'*

Spots, streaks, and splashes of scarlet, pink and orange make Croton a real dazzler. Don't be afraid to put this sun-worshipper in a window that gets lots of direct light—or even outdoors in the summertime if protected overhead from rains.
*Light:* Crotons need at least four hours of very strong light every day, or they'll turn green and lose their rainbow of multihued foliage.
*Temperature range:* 65 to 85 degrees. Drafts or sudden changes in temperature can cause it to drop its lower leaves.
*Special notes:* If a Croton gets leggy during the winter, trim it back in early spring. You'll get a smaller, bushier plant—and you can use the trimmings to start new ones. Propagate by either air-layering or taking stem cuttings, as explained on pages 49 and 45. Red spider mites sometimes take up residence in Crotons.

## Jade Plant
*Crassula argentea*

*Crassula* suffers from something of an identity crisis. Some people call it the Jade Plant, others a Japanese Rubber Plant. Actually, it's not even a distant cousin of the Rubber Tree—and *Crassula* comes from South Africa, not the Orient.

**Peace Lily**
*Spathiphyllum 'Mauna Loa'*

**Croton Elaine**
*Codiaeum 'Elaine'*

You won't have any trouble recognizing those thick, fleshy leaves, though. They resemble inverted thumbs, rounded on the tops, flat underneath. Eventually the Jade Plant assumes the proportions of a small tree, branching out at a height of three feet or more.

*Light:* Jades prefer full sun, but will tolerate bright, indirect light.

*Temperature range:* 50 to 85 degrees is ideal, but these hardy plants can withstand occasional lows of 40 and highs of 100 degrees.

*Special notes:* Jade Plants live for years and aren't especially fussy about their habitats (provided they get enough light). Give one lots of

summer sun and it may produce tiny pink flowers in the autumn. Keep an eye out for scale, mealybugs and edema.

### Ming Aralia or Ming Tree
*Polyscias fruticosa*

Again, don't let the name of this popular indoor shrub confuse you about its origin. Ming Aralias—or Ming Trees as they're sometimes known—come from India, not China. Full-grown specimens reach a height of 1½ to 2 feet, with delicate, willowy leaves and one or more slender trunks.

*Light:* You'll need lots of bright, indirect light for your Ming Tree to thrive.

*Temperature range:* 60 to 85 degrees. Drafts will cause leaf dropping.

*Special notes:* Check periodically for aphids, mealybugs and thrips. You can propagate aralias any time of year with stem cuttings, as explained on page 45.

### Warnecki Dracaena
*Dracaena deremensis 'Warnecki'*

In their native Africa, Warnecki Dracaenas grow to 15 feet. Home versions don't get that tall, of course, but you can expect a sizable plant in just a few years. Fresh green, swordlike foliage, with milky green centers and white, pinstriped margins distinguish Warnecki from other dracaenas.

*Light:* Dracaenas tolerate a variety of light levels, but do best in the medium to high range. Full sun will burn leaves.

*Temperature range:* 60 degrees minimum at night, 85 during the day. Drafts will cause leaves to drop.

*Special notes:* Fluoridated water will burn the tips of leaves, and sometimes even with pure water, tips and edges will discolor; snip off brown spots with scissors. Pests include red spider mites and scale.

You can start new plants by air-layering or with stem cuttings.

**Ming Aralia** or **Ming Tree**
*Polyscias fruticosa*

**Warnecki Dracaena**
*Dracaena deremensis 'Warnecki'*

**Jade Plant**
*Crassula argentea*

## Sweet Boxwood
*Sarcococca ruscifolia*

Like its American cousin on page 64, this native of western China lives just as happily outdoors as in—making it a hardy choice for a chronically cool spot. Put your Sweet Boxwood out on a sheltered patio during the summer months and it'll appreciate the change of scene. A free-branching evergreen, it sports small, oval, leathery leaves. Fragrant, milk-white flowers show up periodically among the lustrous dark green foliage.

*Light:* Medium to high. A few hours of direct sun probably won't hurt, but if leaves begin to yellow or burn, move to a shadier location.

*Temperature range:* Boxwoods aren't fussy and live happily at any temperature between 50 and 85 degrees. Try to avoid drastic fluctuations, though. Most plants have a hard time coping with them.

*Special notes:* Check for scale and mealybugs every so often, especially if you summer the plant outdoors. To propagate, take two- to three-inch cuttings and root them as explained on pages 42 to 48. You may need to mist newly potted cuttings two or three times a day until their roots take hold.

## Chicken Gizzard
*Polyscias 'Chicken Gizzard'*

Leaves that look like something you might find inside Sunday's dinner give this aralia variation its fanciful name. Serve it up with the Celery Leaf Aralia shown on page 71 and garnish with Parsley Ming (page 72) for a visually delicious appetizer.

Chicken can stand on its own, too, preferably against a plain, bright background that plays up its pale green foliage. This version would look good on a windowside table; eventually it will turn into a floor plant, developing an elongated trunk about two feet high.

*Light:* Bright and indirect, please. Aralias like lots of light, but no direct sun. Spindly growth and tiny leaves signal that conditions are too shady. If you simply can't give a plant more sunlight, consider sup-

plementing with artificial light, as explained on pages 24 and 25.

*Temperature range:* 60 to 85 degrees. Like all aralias, Chicken Gizzard can't tolerate drafts. Locate one near a door, cooling or heating register and it'll begin dropping leaves almost immediately.

*Special notes:* Subject to spider mites, scale and thrips. Repot in the spring; start new plants with stem cuttings any time of the year. If a newly potted aralia begins to wilt during dry spells, increase humidity with one of the techniques explained on pages 28 and 29.

## Variegated Peperomia
*Peperomia obtusifolia 'Variegata'*

Yet another lovable Deco favorite, this peperomia plant takes pride in its nuances of color—with chubby, yellow-streaked leaves and crimson stems. These grow to about a foot in height, then fall over and trail down the pot's sides.

Like the Peperomias shown on pages 58 and 59, Variegated is a succulent. This means it stores water for fairly long periods of time and needs to dry out between Nutrient dosings. Add Solution too often and you could have a case of stem rot on your hands. After the visual Moisture Level Indicator drops to its lowest point, wait a few days before refilling.

*Light:* Medium to bright, but no direct sun. The stronger the light, the more vivid the leaf markings will be.

*Temperature range:* 60 degrees minimum, 80 degrees tops.

*Special notes:* You can propagate by rooting leaf cuttings, but the new

plant will be all green, without those characteristic splashes of yellow. To retain them, divide the roots, as explained on page 49. Or, use three to four leaf "tip cuttings."

Most pests won't bother Peperomias, but keep an eye out for ring spot, a virus infection. This shows up as concentric rings on the leaves, and growth may be stunted as well. If your Variegated Peperomia comes down with a case of it, resign yourself to throwing the plant out.

## Abidjan Rubber Tree
*Ficus 'Abidjan'*

Abidjan is the capital city of the Ivory Coast, in western Africa—a densely forested region that gets lots of rainfall. This explains why the Rubber Trees that grow there like weeds have tough, furrowed leaves. The furrows act as gutters that channel excess water to a tapered, dropping "drip tip."

The soilfree Deco Plantsystem helps make sure you don't overwater a Deco Abidjan—but those big leaves make for a houseplant that's as hardy as it is handsome.

**Chicken Gizzard**
*Polyscias 'Chicken Gizzard'*

**Sweet Boxwood**
*Sarcococca ruscifolia*

**Abidjan Rubber Tree**
*Ficus 'Abidjan'*

**Variegated Peperomia**
*Peperomia obtusfolia 'Variegata'*

**Canary Island Ivy**
*Hedera canariensis variegata*

With only minimal care it'll grow for years, reaching the ceiling if you don't periodically cut back its growing tip.

*Light* Medium to high. No direct sun. Poor light weakens the leaf stems, making them fragile and prone to breaking off.

*Temperature range* 55 to 85 degrees. Station a Rubber Tree in a drafty spot and you'll end up with a sorry specimen like the one shown on page 27. Avoid abrupt temperature changes, too.

*Special notes:* To maintain the leaves' rich, deep, sheen, wipe them periodically with a damp cloth. Propagate by rooting stem cuttings—or shorten an Abidjan that's grown too tall by air-layering. And be on the lookout for thrips and foliar nematodes.

### Canary Island Ivy
*Hedera canariensis variegata*

A variation of the English-type ivies shown on pages 52, 54, 66 and 67, this Mediterranean native has most of the same characteristics. It climbs like a monkey, trails just as readily, and prefers coolish temperatures. But like most variegated plants, Canary Island Ivy needs brighter light than its parents can get by on.

*Light* Medium to high. To maintain the brilliance of those creamy edge markings, supply bright light—but no direct sun. *Temperature range:* 55 to 60 degrees in the winter, under 80 in the summer. Warm, dry conditions encourage spider mites.

*Special notes:* Like all ivies, this one is especially easy to root with leaf or tip cuttings. Give plants a rest during their dormant period—December to February—by giving them less Nutrient Solution and cooler temperatures. Be especially vigilant for spider mites. Cyclamen mites and scale can be problems, too.

63

**Weeping Fig**
*Ficus benjamina*

**California Boxwood**
*Buxus microphylla japonica*

**White Zebra Plant**
*Aphelandra 'Silver Cloud'*

## Weeping Fig
### Ficus benjamina

No, there's nothing especially sad about this Indian fruit tree. The nickname goes back to the reason it was originally cultivated—for its sap. Full-grown *F. benjaminas* have graceful branches drooping from a single trunk. With proper light, they reach a height of six to eight feet and live almost indefinitely.

*Light:* High light and even a touch of direct sun keep Weeping Fig in good health. If conditions are too dim, leaves will begin to drop off. (Come to the rescue in time and new ones will sprout shortly.)

*Temperature range:* For best growth, maintain levels of 65 to 85 degrees; avoid drops below 55 degrees and abrupt temperature changes.

*Special notes:* Its size and graceful, treelike proportions make *F. benjamina* a solo plant, one that can be the focal point of any room. To start a new plant, root stem cuttings as shown on page 45. Pests include scale and thrips.

## California Boxwood
### Buxus microphylla japonica

Most houseplants come from tropical climes and don't take kindly to cool temperatures. Not so the native American Boxwood. Larger specimens of this hardy evergreen have long served as outdoor shrubbery and are often shaped by pruning into geometric shapes. Indoors, this dwarf version makes an excellent choice for a chilly or drafty spot that's been the death of warmer-blooded plants.

*Light:* Medium to high. Boxwoods also don't mind a few hours of direct sunlight.

*Temperature range:* 50 to 85 degrees. Don't worry if the thermometer occasionally dips into the 40s.

*Special notes:* Boxwood's enemies include mealybugs and scale.

## White Zebra Plant
### Aphelandra 'Silver Cloud'

One look at this one's boldly striped foliage tells you where its common name comes from. Maintain its fairly rigorous growing conditions and the Zebra Plant will also reward you with dramatic spikes of waxy yellow or gold flowers in spring, summer, and sometimes fall, as well. Individual blooms don't last long, but the spikes continue elongating and flowering for weeks at a time.

*Light:* Like most flowering plants, the Zebra needs high light levels—but keep it away from full sun or the leaves will scorch.

*Temperature range:* On the cool side, 55 to 80 degrees. Keep it away from drafts—especially air conditioners.

*Special notes:* Your *Aphelandra* may get leggy in the winter, after it's finished flowering. If this happens, start a new one by rooting a four- to six-inch cutting (see pages 44 and 45.) Watch out for red spiders, aphids, broad mites and thrips.

## Marble Peperomia
*Peperomia obtusifolia 'Marble'*

Irregular splotches of color on its deep green leaves set this peperomia plant apart from its hundreds of cousins. It tops off at 8 to 10 inches high. Don't be alarmed if mature plants suddenly lean over; they tend to trail when full grown, making them good candidates for hanging situations or the edge of a tabletop. To learn about three other types of peperomia, turn to pages 59 and 63.

*Light:* Medium to high, but no direct sun, please. A north or west window is ideal, though west light should be filtered in summer.

*Temperature range:* 60 to 80 degrees.

*Special notes:* Propagate new plants with stem cuttings (see page 45). Subject to edema, a rot that occurs at or below the pot line; if your peperomia has it, take cuttings to start a new plant and discard the old one.

## Spineless Yucca
*Yucca elephantipes*

Sharp, rigid, bayonet-like leaves—10 to 18 inches long—defend the Yucca against enemies in the jungles of Mexico and Guatemala. There this tree often reaches a height of 20 feet, with closely grouped clusters of foliage spaced along a woody, cane-like trunk.

An indoor Yucca also will eventually develop one or more trunks, topping out at four to six feet. Use one as a solitary accent, or let it tower over smaller plants—just be sure to locate it where people or plants won't brush against those prickly points. They hurt!

*Light:* A Yucca needs medium to high light intensities if it's to thrive.

*Temperature range:* 60 degrees nighttime, up to 85 during the day. Tolerates air conditioning but not direct drafts.

*Special notes:* Subject to thrips. Fluoridated water can burn the tips of leaves. If growth gets out of hand, simply saw off a trunk at four to six inches above the top of the container. New growth will sprout from the stump.

**Spineless Yucca**
*Yucca elephantipes*

**Marble Peperomia**
*Peperomia obtusifolia 'Marble'*

65

### Schefflera or Umbrella Tree
*Brassaia actinophylla*

Scheffleras are often called "umbrella trees." Examine this one's canopied leaves and handle-like stems, and you can see why. The broad leaf foliage makes Schefflera an excellent shade tree in its native Queensland.

This is an easy-care floor plant that grows slowly to a height of six feet or more. Young Scheffleras have three glossy green leaflets in each cluster; older ones develop five or more.

If your Schefflera threatens to get too big for its surroundings, reduce its size by air layering (see page 49).
*Light:* Provide plenty of bright light, but no direct sun.
*Temperature range:* Schefflera prefers a warm, 60- to 85-degree room.
*Special notes:* Dust or wash the shiny foliage often so the plant can breathe properly. When you do this, always support each leaf from underneath; they snap off easily. You can propagate with stem cuttings or air-layering. Pests: red spider mites, aphids and scale.

### Ribbon Plant
*Dracaena sanderiana*

Also known as Sander's Dracaena (for the man who first classified it), the Ribbon Plant's elongated leaves make a colorful fountain of green and white stripes. To visualize this one's place of origin, think of drumbeats, gold mines and the lush jungles of the Congo.

Like many dracaenas, the Ribbon Plant eventually begins to rise on one or more ringed, canelike trunks. To keep a plant in shape, cut back the canes when growth gets out of hand. Just saw off a trunk at four to six inches above the pot line. New growth will spring from the stump's sides.
*Light:* Ribbon Plants can tolerate low levels, but medium to high intensities promote growth. No direct sun, please.
*Temperature range:* 60 to 85 degrees. Protect against drafts.

*Special notes:* If water in your community is heavily fluoridated, mix Nutrient with bottled or rain water to prevent tip burning. Even with pure water you may get browning at edges and tips. Cut away brown spots with scissors to maintain a healthy look. Check every so often for red spider mites.

### Needlepoint Ivy
*Hedera helix 'Needlepoint'*

Ivy is ivy, right? Wrong! There are dozens of different varieties of this household plant, and some aren't even distantly related.

Needlepoint is a true ivy, a member of the *Hedera* genus and named for its pointed, three-lobed leaf. According to one legend, if Needlepoint dies, its owner will lose his or her home.

You needn't worry about foreclosure, though. Needlepoint is a hardy specimen and will live almost indefinitely, provided you

**Ribbon Plant**
*Dracaena sanderiana*

**Schefflera or Umbrella Tree**
*Brassaia actinophylla*

**Needlepoint Ivy**
*Hedera helix 'Needlepoint'*

answer its simple needs for medium to bright light and slightly coolish temperatures.

*Light:* The more the better, but no direct sun.

*Temperature range:* 55 to 80 degrees. Occasional lows in the 40s and highs of 85 won't hurt.

*Special notes:* Cut down the Nutrient level during the short days of winter so plants can get a good rest. Increase the dosage in February or March. Lower winter temperatures are beneficial, too. To start new vines, take six-to-eight-inch cuttings, remove a couple of lower leaves, and root as explained on page 45. Pests include scale and cyclamen mites.

## Golden Pothos or Devil's Ivy
*Epipremnum aureum*

The first of this one's common names may have to do with the fact that it's a fooler. Sometimes mistaken for philodendron, sometimes considered a true ivy, it's really neither. Nevertheless, since Pothos climbs and trails as well as the *Hedera* types shown on either side of it, treat it just about the same as you would any ivy.

*Light:* Medium to high. It can tolerate slightly lower levels than Needlepoint or English Ivy.

*Temperature range:* This native of the Solomon Islands doesn't mind the heat—55 to 85 degrees.

*Special notes:* Grows rapidly, especially in strong light. Train tendrils to climb a trellis or support and pinch them back when they reach the top. Root cuttings as described for Needlepoint Ivy (at left). Watch out for thrips, mealybugs and red spider mites.

## English Ivy
*Hedera helix*

And now meet the truest of the true ivies. English is the parent from which other forms—such as Needlepoint (opposite page), Sweetheart (page 52), Holly (page 54) and Canary Island (page 62) derive. Contrast its small, forest green leaves with those on Devil's Ivy just to its left.

Versatile English Ivy loves to climb just about anything; however, it'll just as happily trail from a hanging pot. For an especially bushy table plant, cut back shoots as soon as they try to leave the pot; you'll get a dense, dark-green mass of foliage.

*Light:* English Ivy can survive in low light, but for better growth, provide medium to high levels.

*Temperature range:* On the cool side. During the winter, 55 to 60 degrees is ideal. Summer temperatures shouldn't exceed 80.

*Special notes:* As with Needlepoint, cut down Nutrient during the darkest days of winter. Propagate as you would any ivy. Scale—and especially cyclamen mites—can be a problem with English Ivy.

**English Ivy**
*Hedera helix*

**Golden Pothos** or **Devil's Ivy**
*Epipremnum aureum*

**Rubber Tree**
*Ficus elastica 'Robusta'*

**Variegated Chinese Evergreen** or **Silver Evergreen**
*Aglaonema commutatum elegans*

## Rubber Tree
*Ficus Elastica 'Robusta'*

Native to India, this well-known indoor tree is a dwarf version of the very same one that natural rubber comes from. There, specimens grow to 100 feet tall and produce a milky sap you probably know as latex; household types could eventually reach the ceiling if you let them, but don't expect one to yield a cash crop.

*Light:* Some persons may try to assure you that a Rubber Tree will thrive in the poorest light. Don't believe them! In its natural environment, this towering giant gets full sun. You should provide medium to high indirect light. The plant can even withstand some direct sun.

*Temperature range:* 55 to 85 degrees. No drafts, please.

*Special notes:* When your Rubber Tree reaches the height you like—or gets too straggly for your taste—cut off its growing point with a sharp knife. The plant will stop its upward progress and send out side shoots instead. And if you'd like to start a new tree, air-layer the tip before cutting it off as explained on page 49. Rubber trees are occasionally attacked by thrips.

## Variegated Chinese Evergreen or Silver Evergreen
*Aglaonema commutatum elegans*

With splashes of gray on his leathery leaves, this distinguished gent—sometimes called Silver Evergreen—is a bit flashier than his plain green cousin shown on page 52. He doesn't grow quite as tall, either, topping off at about a foot, compared to twice that height for ordinary Chinese Evergreens.

*Light:* This plant tolerates a wide range of intensities—from low to high—but not direct sun. Markings will fade somewhat, however, in low light conditions.

*Temperature range:* 65 to 85 degrees. Protect from drafts, and don't set the plant too close to a window on cold winter nights.

*Special notes:* You can propagate

Silver Evergreens by either dividing mature plants or by rooting stem cuttings. Check for mealybugs, scale and virus infection.

## Compact Dracaena
*Dracaena deremensis 'Compacta'*

If you like the long-leafed look of a dracaena but don't have space for one of these normally towering plants, consider this dwarf version of the Janet Craig shown on page 55. Bushier than most of its relatives, the *Compacta* rarely gets taller than a foot or so, making it perfect for a tabletop or window ledge.
*Light:* Medium to high. Shield from direct sun.
*Temperature range:* 60 to 85 degrees.
*Special notes:* All dracaenas appreciate having their leaves washed every so often. Dust and dirt impede breathing. Watch out for scale; fluoridated water can burn the tips of leaves.

## Balfour Aralia
*Polyscias balfouriana 'Marginata'*

The South Pacific territory of New Caledonia is a series of lush islands where aralia trees like this one reach a height of 20 feet or more. Indoors, it will eventually top out at four to six feet, provided you maintain the relatively high levels of light it needs.

White halos around Balfour's earlike leaves distinguish it from other aralias. Note, too, that several different, unrelated plant species are commonly sold as aralias.
*Light:* Balfour does its best with high, indirect light. Under low light, it may drop leaves; full sun can burn them.
*Temperature range:* 60 to 85 degrees. Drafts can cause leaf loss.
*Special notes:* Red spider mites, scale and thrips are common pests.

## Corn Plant
*Dracaena fragrans 'Massangeana'*

Not only does *D. fragrans* look like a stalk of corn, it grows just about as tall—six feet or more. Its botanical name refers to the fact that under just the right growing conditions, *D. fragrans* will blossom and perfume the air with its scent.
*Light:* Medium to high. This plant also does well under fluorescent grow-lights. It will tolerate low light levels, but will grow slowly and leaves may lose their characteristic yellow stripes.
*Temperature range:* 60 to 85 degrees.
*Special notes:* Mature specimens sometimes send up several stalks. To keep them symmetrical, cut back the taller ones. Subject to scale. Fluoride in the water can burn the tips of leaves.

**Corn Plant**
*Dracaena fragrans 'Massangeana'*

**Compact Dracaena**
*Dracaena deremensis 'Compacta'*

**Balfour Aralia**
*Polyscias balfouriana 'Marginata'*

## Dieffenbachia or Dumb Cane
*Dieffenbachia 'Exotica Perfection'*

Dumb Cane might make an excellent gift for a meddlesome mother-in-law. Its unusual common name refers to an equally unusual property of the sap from its leaves and stem. Get some in the mouth or throat and it may temporarily paralyze vocal cords, rendering the victim speechless.

(That's why you should be careful not to put fingers in your mouth or eyes after handling this plant—and keep it well away from small children and pets; for them the sap could be seriously harmful or even fatal.)

Dumb Cane hails from Columbia, and boasts large, deep green leaves that have cream-colored blotches emanating from their ribs. It tops out at about four feet and makes an excellent choice to fill an open floor space.

*Light:* Though Dumb Cane can survive in light so low that your hand barely casts a shadow, you'll get best results in medium to high light. Direct sun will turn Dumb Cane's foliage yellow.

*Temperature range:* 65 degrees night, 85 during the day.

*Special notes:* This resilient plant does better when you neglect it a bit. When the Nutrient indicator drops to the bottom, wait a day or two before adding more solution. Don't leave Dumb Cane dry too long, though, or its leaves will discolor.

When growth gets too leggy, cut it off several inches above the ground and root the stem. Keep the potted roots, too; they'll send up a new cane from the stub. You can also propagate by air-layering, as shown on page 49. Dumb Canes are subject to red spider mites and virus infection.

## Red-margined Dracaena or Madagascar Dragon Tree
*Dracaena marginata*

Imagine what a dragon's tongue might look like and you can see where this plant got its common name. The Dragon Tree's long, slender leaves are edged with thin coppery stripes, making it a dramatic accent plant.

As with some other dracaenas, *D. marginata* loses its lower leaves as it grows, revealing an angular stem that can be shaped with florist's wire or strong directional light. Eventually this sculptural beauty will reach a height of six feet or more, growing about a foot a year.

**Red-margined Dracaena** or
**Madagascar Dragon Tree**
*Dracaena marginata*

**Dieffenbachia** or **Dumb Cane**
*Dieffenbachia 'Exotica Perfection'*

*Light:* Medium to high intensities. The brighter the light, the more vivid the plant's coloring will be. Avoid direct sun, though.

*Temperature range:* 60 to 85 degrees. Tolerates air conditioning fairly well, but keep out of drafts.

*Special notes:* Cutting off the top will cause new clusters of leaves to sprout from the stalk. These will show up in three to four weeks. You can propagate a new plant with stem cuttings, or by air-layering (see pages 45 and 49). Wipe the leaves clean periodically with a damp cloth to promote breathing.

Fluoridated water can burn *D. marginata's* tips. Some browning at the edges and tips is normal, however; just cut away the discolorations. Keep an eye out for red spider mites, which seem to be quite fond of dracaenas.

## Celery Leaf Aralia
*Polyscias guilfoylei*

Display this aralia against a plain background to bring out its graceful branches and delicate leaves. Or better yet, stand it in front of a sheer-curtained window. You'll get a good look at the lacy foliage, and the plant will appreciate the bright light it's used to getting in its native land of Polynesia.

There, specimens grow into full-size trees, upwards of 20 feet high. You can expect yours to mature at four to five feet.

*Light:* The Celery Leaf needs lots of it, but direct sun will burn leaves and cause them to drop.

*Temperature range:* 60 at night, 85 maximum during the day. Avoid temperatures below 55 and drafts, which can cause leaf drop.

**Celery Leaf Aralia**
*Polyscias guilfoylei*

**Tricolor Wax Plant**
*Hoya carnosa 'Tricolor'*

*Special notes:* Let the plant dry out somewhat before replenishing its Nutrient Solution. Otherwise, the roots could rot. If you decide to increase its size by repotting in a bigger container, do this job in the spring. You can propagate any time of the year with stem cuttings, as explained on page 45. Beware of scale and thrips.

## Tricolor Wax Plant
*Hoya carnosa 'Tricolor'*

Add a *Hoya* to your indoor garden and you can expect people to ask, "Is it real?" Ablaze with color all year long, its thick, shiny leaves seem to be made of wax. And as if the leaves aren't dazzling enough, the plant also sends out fragrant, star-shaped flowers in the spring and early summer.

Originally cultivated in China for the emperors' gardens, the Wax Plant is a climber that likes to have a trellis it can get a foothold on. Or, hang one overhead and let its brilliant foliage add a new dimension to any planting area. Prune little, if at all.

*Light:* Medium to high, the brighter the light, the more color. Let the plant go dormant in the winter, though, by moving it to a low-light situation. In February, return to a bright intensity. Be sure to filter direct sunlight.

*Temperature range:* Coolish in winter; about 55 degrees is ideal. Warmer in the summer—up to about 80 degrees.

*Special notes:* Let the plant dry slightly between Nutrient feedings in the spring and summer, even longer in late fall and early winter. This encourages Tricolor to bloom the following spring. After flowers have bloomed, don't remove their spurs, as next year's buds rise from these.

To start new plants, take four- to six-inch stem cuttings at any time of year; cut just below a pair or group of leaves. Expect to wait a year or two before a new *Hoya* blooms. The Wax Plant's principal enemies include mealybugs, aphids and thrips (see pages 35 to 39).

71

## Parsley Ming or Bonsai Aralia
*Polyscias fruticosa 'Elegans'*

Delicate, parsley-like leaves make this variety of *Polyscias* look almost good enough to eat. Sometimes called a Bonsai Aralia, it resembles the Ming Tree shown on page 61. Parsley Ming is a bit more compact and bushy, though, and has smaller, darker green foliage.

To learn about a couple of other "aralias" (*Polyscias* is actually their correct name), see pages 69 and 71.
*Light:* Like any aralia, Parsley Ming needs lots of bright, filtered light. In shady locations it will lose leaves and eventually die. Direct sun can do damage, too.
*Temperature range:* 60 to 85 degrees. Avoid drafts and prolonged exposure to levels below 55 degrees. Again, when an aralia drops leaves, it's trying to tell you that something is wrong with its environment.
*Special notes:* Repot in the spring. You can start new plants any time of the year with stem cuttings (see page 45). Inspect regularly for aphids, mealybugs, scale and thrips (see pages 35 to 39).

## Snake Plant or
## Mother-in-law's Tongue
*Sansevieria trifasciata 'Laurenti'*

One look at the long, thick, tough leaves of this variety of *Sansevieria* tells you where its common name comes from. Mottled green and edged with yellow stripes, they resemble a deadly snake—and indeed you might find one lurking among them in this plant's native habitat, the northeastern Congo.

The leaves rise from short, underground branches called rhizomes, and grow to a height of 18 to 24 inches. A mature plant will also send up spikes of dainty, white fragrant blossoms every so often.
*Light:* Snake Plants exist happily in dim corners, but do even better in bright, indirect light. Avoid full sun, though; it will burn the leaves.
*Special notes:* Just about as tough as an old snake, *Sansevieria* will withstand almost any abuse—low light, low humidity, drafts, heat and dust—but a bit of pampering will reward you with lush vigorous

growth. Wash its leaves every so often, and cut down on Nutrient Solution during the plant's dormant period in the fall and early winter. Start new ones by dividing the rhizomes of old plants—or take leaf cuttings. Be warned, though, that leaf cuttings may produce all-green leaves—not the variegated *Sansevieria* plants.

## Wax Plant or Hoya
*Hoya carnosa 'Rubra'*

Though not quite as flashy as her tricolored sister shown on the preceding page, *Rubra's* gold and green leaves still make a strong showing in any plant grouping. Set this semisucculent vine on a table and let it trail over the edge, or train it to climb a pole or trellis. After the plant matures, you can expect waxy white blossoms to appear in the spring and early summer months.
*Light:* Put *Rubra* near a window that receives medium to strong indirect or diffused light. The stronger the light, the more brilliant her markings will be.
*Temperature range:* Keep warm in summer, cooler in the winter. 55 to 80 degrees is about right.
*Special notes:* Cut down Nutrient Solution levels (and light) in late fall and early winter—providing just enough to keep the leaves from shriveling—and you'll be rewarded with more blossoms in the spring. To start new plants, take four- to six-inch cuttings from just below a pair or group of leaves. They'll root easily in five to six weeks. Keep a close watch for thrips, aphids—and especially mealybugs. These pests can be particularly hard to dig out of the Hoya's twisting stems.

## Arrowhead or Cream Nephthytis
*Syngonium podophyllum 'Cream'*

From Mexico and Costa Rica, Cream Arrowhead has leaves as green as guacamole and floppy as an old sombrero. Given time, this slow-growing cousin of the philodendron develops vines that can turn your house into a verdant hacienda. But first, Arrowhead—also known as Cream Nephthytis—sends up a series of

stalks that can reach a height of two feet before they fall over or begin to climb a support.
*Light:* Medium to high levels, such as you'd get from an east or sunny west window. No direct sun.
*Temperature range:* 60 to 85 degrees. Avoid sudden temperature changes.
*Special notes:* To slow growth, pinch back new shoots. When a plant gets leggy, start a new one with stem cuttings and discard the parent. Thrips sometimes attack *Syngonium*, and it's subject to bacterial leafspot.

## Grape Ivy
*Cissus rhombifolia*

Although not strictly an ivy (see the discussion on pages 66 and 67), this easy-growing vine is a member of the grape family, with soft brown stems, coiling tendrils and metallic green, quilted leaves.

A native of the West Indies, Grape Ivy is happy at normal indoor temperatures, and has a moderate to rapid growth rate. Like the Cream Nephthytis in front of it here, *Cissus* stands erect until it's about two feet high, then cascades over the side of the container.
*Light:* Moderate to high is best, but Grape Ivy doesn't need as much as some other types. Direct sun will wilt leaves.
*Temperature range:* 55 to 80 degrees. Don't worry if the thermometer dips below 55 occasionally, but protect against cold drafts, such as you might get from air conditioning registers.
*Special notes:* To encourage branching, pinch back tips. Provide a pole or trellis and Grape Ivy will be delighted to climb it. Like most ivies, this popular plant is easy to root with stem cuttings. Take six- to eight-inch lengths of medium mature growth, remove several of the lower leaves, and root in water, as shown on page 45. Scale and especially red spider mites can attack Grape Ivy. Salts can build up more rapidly than with other plants, too, so leach the Living Stones more frequently.

**Parsley Ming** or **Bonsai Aralia**
*Polyscias fruticosa 'Elegans'*

**Grape Ivy**
*Cissus rhombifolia*

**Snake Plant** or
**Mother-in-law's Tongue**
*Sansevieria trifasciata 'Laurenti'*

**Arrowhead** or **Cream Nephthytis**
*Syngonium podophyllum 'Cream'*

**Wax Plant** or **Hoya**
*Hoya carnosa 'Rubra'*

73

# CHAPTER 6

# Solve your decorating problems with plants

First on our tour of well-decorated homes: the living room. Color yours with greenery, as we did here (compare with "before" picture below). Plants love human voices, so be sure to include them—whether one or a dozen in any conversation area.

# Don't stop with the living room... plants add excitement to any area of your home

Kitchens, family rooms, baths, studies, bedrooms, entries, breakfast areas. . . it's hard to imagine any part of your home that green, growing things can't turn into a fresher, more natural-feeling environment. Different plants have differing light, humidity and temperature needs, of course—so in designing this trio of appealing examples, we've chosen species you can be sure will do well in locations like these.

**Splash a bath with greenery.** Thirsty plants—such as the Golden Pothos and Heart-leaf Philodendron flanking the mirror, as well as the Marble Queen atop the flush tank—will appreciate the humidity. And a mini-slat window blind lets you adjust light levels to suit them and the English Ivy in the foreground. Deco wall hangers make it easy to sprinkle greenery in small quarters.

**Wake up your breakfast area with a window garden.** It'll be just as inviting at lunch and dinnertime—or any hour you feel like a cup of coffee. Gardens like this one grow slowly—you add a plant or two at a time. You might start with the Danica and Grape Ivies in the window, later add the Dieffenbachia, Ficus Benjamina, Janet Craig Dracaena, Rubber Tree and Green Emerald. Then, fill out the area with the Palm, Silver King and second Dieffenbachia at near right. Stagger heights so every plant gets good light.

**An antique-store "find" makes a mellow place** to array tabletop plants. Just situate your treasure near a window (but out of direct sun) and load it up with Deco favorites. This rolltop garden even turns paying the monthly bills into a refreshing experience. A couple coats of polyurethane protect the desk against occasional watering mishaps.

77

## Give your place a warm, homey feeling with plants

No law says you *have* to mass greenery in only a few locations. Often, in fact, you can get more decorating mileage by separating your favorite plants from the crowd and letting them stand alone or in smaller groupings—just as they do in nature. Here are some examples that show a few of the ways you can use Deco Plants to spread a little sunshine throughout your home.

**Perk up a dull stairway.** Like many stairways, this one (upper left) had a ho-hum air. Four Deco Plants changed all that. On the landing, a curtained window provides the strong, filtered light our Peace Lily likes best. A multi-leveled Hawaiian Schefflera, Grape Ivy and Silver King Evergreen enhance the lackluster area at the foot of the stairs.

**Cool down a warm color scheme.** Wood tones, browns, golds and other earthy hues might have been too much for this family room (lower left)—if we hadn't cooled the scene with restful touches of green. In low-light situations you may need to supplement natural light with table lamps or spotlights— or rotate plants to brighter areas frequently.

**Make a window treatment** that's as handy as it is surprising by hanging often-used utensils in a kitchen garden like the one shown below. All you need is a supported rod above and a single shelf below—and you have the perfect spot for African Violets, Ming Aralias and other showy plants. Use skinny window blinds to easily adjust light intensities.

# Create a view with plants...ways with windows

How's the outlook at your house? Most of us have a few windows with views that are less than inspiring. Where there's nothing much to look at outside, focus your attention on an indoor Deco garden. Here are two approaches.

**Provide privacy with plants and shutters.** Check the *inset* photograph at left and you'll see that this bedroom window looked right at a neighboring house. Now, some inexpensive pine shutters nicely filter light for a bevy of plants—swapping the bad view for an attention-getting focal point. Adjustable louvers let you fine-tune both light and privacy levels. Note how the Deco Plant leather hanger at far left holds two containers.

**Set up ladders for a successful** (and portable) window garden. This treatment (below) works especially well in apartments and homes with sliding glass doors. Come spring, when you want to use the doors again, it all dismantles in minutes.

# Use plants as a focal point

Have you ever been in a room that seems well-dressed, but somehow it doesn't quite come off? Chances are it lacked a focal point—a center of attention that catches the eye. Fortunately, focal points aren't difficult to create. All you need is an eyeful of Deco Plants.

**Give an end table a new beginning** with a plant grouping such as the one shown at upper left. Here, a Marble Queen, Chinese Evergreen and Silver King not only add interest, but they also bring cool color to a warm-toned corner. The lamp—which almost seems to be growing itself—supplements the natural light.

**Fill a fireplace with foliage.** In wintertime, a crackling fire makes a compelling focal point. Come spring, when the last embers have cooled, move in your favorite Deco Plants to hold your attention all summer long. The one shown (lower left) gets inadequate light, so we rotate plants to a brighter spot every few days.

**Rescue an empty corner.** Imagine the area pictured below without any plants in it and you'll realize just how much life they add to the situation. Here, greenery not only fills bland, vacant space, but it also helps to bring the outdoors in through those big windows. For a couple of additional attention-getters, turn to pages 86 and 87.

# Assemble plants for a dramatic effect

What makes plants so fascinating to look at is their almost endless variety . . . a rhapsody in green that delights with hundreds of different hues, shapes, sizes and textures. Try playing these differences against each other and you'll soon discover how much fun it is to make visual music with plants—in groupings ranging from a duet to a symphony. These ideas should get you started.

**Mass lots and lots of foliage** and it's hard to go wrong. With a dozen different species, the bedroom jungle on the opposite page can hardly help but be striking. And it's easy to create additional interest by varying the colors of Deco containers, sheathing them in wood or wicker, or potting the Soilfree Deco Plant-system in a ceramic container.

**For a portable accent, plant a basket.** Actually, almost any inexpensive container will do—as long as it has room for your favorite Deco Plants. Just set in the pots and arrange them to suit yourself. To protect wood or wicker against moisture spills, spray with a sealer. Or, line the inside with plastic or aluminum foil.

**Make a centerpiece with plants.** Why pay a florist for a flower arrangement that will last only a few days? Assemble a grouping of flowering and unflowering Deco Plants—like the African Violets, ivy and Heart-leaf Philodendron shown at left. Dinner parties at your house will be blooming for many months and many years to come.

85

# Round out corners with plants

Somewhere in almost every home or apartment lurks a do-nothing corner. No matter what you try to put into it—furnishings, art, accessories—the space just looks back at you with a dull, dead stare. The answer? You guessed it! Soften those bleak angles with a few curvaceous plants.

**Enliven an already-busy corner.** Check the photograph *below* and you'll see a scheme that already seems to have everything going for it . . . yet its atmosphere is just a little too cool and studied to be really inviting. Now, move in a few Deco Plants, and look at the difference (opposite page). Varying textures—from the Danica Ivy in the window to the Norfolk Island Pine on the floor—bring it all to life.

**Or, fill an empty corner.** In this bedroom (above) there's hardly space for furniture in the corner, but a Hawaiian Schefflera accommodates itself nicely, as do the Grape Ivy in the hanger, Variegated Peperomia on the table, and Silver King Evergreen on the floor. Here, again, shutters enable you to modulate light levels, and the table lamp helps the Peperomia out with the higher light intensity it needs.

# Accent collectibles with plants

Do you have a collection that's collecting nothing but dust? If so, maybe now's the time to get out those treasures and show them off. Exactly how you choose to display collectibles depends to some extent, of course, on what they are . . . but a few splashes of greenery add freshness and excitement to almost any arrangement. Here's a trio of Deco-Planted ideas you can feel free to borrow or adapt.

**Play up a wall grouping.** Mushrooms are one family's hobby, so they incorporated them into a dining room wall treatment (right), then interspersed their finds with plants that add to the collection's natural air. Deco wall brackets make this one especially easy to accomplish.

**Set off a rock or shell collection** with various plant textures. In the photograph at the bottom of the opposite page, a Snake Plant, several Peperomias, a Jade, Hoya and Dieffenbachia add color and dimension to a scattering of seashells. Red clay drain tiles lend even more contrast. Stack them any way you wish.

**Stage everything on shelves.** A wicker éta-gère exhibits a collection of American Indian art and artifacts (right), made all the more dramatic by a few well-chosen Deco Plants. On top is a Red-veined Prayer Plant, then a Corn Plant, Ming Aralia, two Peperomias on the bottom shelf, and a Yucca on the floor. Spotlights show off the collection as well as supplement lighting for the plants—a combination certain to brighten a shady wall.

# Appendix

## Deco Plants at a glance

How much light does your plant need? What are its temperature preferences? Who are its enemies? What are its common and scientific plant names? For fast answers, consult these pages. And to learn more about each of the Deco Plants listed here, see the detailed profiles on pages 52 through 73.

---

**Abidjan Rubber Tree** (*Ficus 'Abidjan'*). Light: medium to high. Temperature: 55-85 degrees. Pests: thrips, foliar nematodes.

**African Violet** (*Saintpaulia ionantha*). Light: low. Temperature: 65-85 degrees. Pests: Cyclaman mites, mealybugs.

**Arrowhead** or **Cream Nephthytis** (*Syngonium podophyllum 'Cream'*). Light: medium to high. Temperature: 60-85 degrees. Pests: bacterial leafspot.

**Arrowhead Vine** or **Variegated Nephthytis** (*Syngonium podophyllum 'Roxanne'*). Light: medium to high. Temperature: 60-85 degrees. Pests: thrips, bacterial leafspot.

**Balfour Aralia** (*Polyscias balfouriana 'Marginata'*). Light: high. Temperature: 60-85 degrees. Pests: spider mites, scale, thrips.

**California Boxwood** (*Buxus microphylla japonica*). Light: medium to high. Temperature: 50-85 degrees. Pests: mealybugs, scale.

**Canary Island Ivy** (*Hedera canariensis variegata*). Light: medium to high. Temperature: 55-80 degrees. Pests: spider mites, cyclamen mites.

**Celery Leaf Aralia** (*Polyscias guilfolei*). Light: high. Temperature: 60-85 degrees. Pests: scale, thrips.

**Chicken Gizzard** (*Polyscias 'Chicken Gizzard'*). Light: bright indirect. Temperature: 60-85 degrees. Pests: spider mites, scale, thrips.

**Chinese Evergreen** (*Aglaonema modestum*). Light: low to high. Temperature: 65-85 degrees. Pests: mealybugs, scale, virus.

**Compact Dracaena** (*Dracaena deremensis 'Compacta'*). Light: medium to high. Temperature: 60-85 degrees. Pests: scale.

**Corn Plant** (*Dracaena fragrans 'Massangeana'*). Light: medium to high. Temperature: 60-85 degrees. Pests: scale.

**Croton Elaine** (*Codiaeum 'Elaine'*). Light: high. Temperature: 65-85 degrees. Pests: spider mites.

**Cupid Peperomia** (*Peperomia scandens 'Variegata'*). Light: medium to high. Temperature: 60-80 degrees.

**Danica Ivy** (*Cissus 'Ellen Danica'*). Light: medium to high. Temperature: 60-85 degrees. Pests: spider mites.

**Dieffenbachia** or **Dumbcane** (*Dieffenbachia x 'Exotica Perfection'*). Light: low. Temperature: 65-85 degrees. Pests: spider mites, virus.

**English Ivy** (*Hedera helix*). Light: medium to high. Temperature: 55-60 degrees. Pests: scale, cyclamen mites.

**Gold Dust Dracaena** (*Dracaena godseffiana*). Light: medium to high. Temperature: 60-85 degrees. Pests: spider mites.

**Golden Pothos** or **Devil's Ivy** (*Epipremnum aureum*). Light: medium to high. Temperature: 55-85 degrees. Pests: thrips, mealybugs, spider mites.

**Grape Ivy** (*Cissus rhombifolia*). Light: medium to high. Temperature: 55-80 degrees. Pests: scale, spider mites.

**Green Emerald Philodendron** (*Philodendron x 'Green Emerald'*). Light: medium to high. Temperature: 60-85 degrees. Pests: virus, scale, spider mites, bacterial leafspot.

**Green Peperomia** (*Peperomia obtusifolia*). Light: medium to high. Temperature: 60-80 degrees. Pests: virus.

**Hawaiian Schefflera** (*Brassaia arboricola*). Light: medium to high. Temperature: 55-85 degrees. Pests: scale, aphids.

**Heart-leaf Philodendron** (*Philodendron scandens oxycardium*). Light: low to high. Temperature: 55-85 degrees. Pests: thrips.

**Holly Ivy** (*Hedera helix 'Holly'*). Light: medium to high. Temperature: 55-80 degrees. Pests: cyclamen mites and scale.

**Jade Plant** (*Crassula argentea*). Light: high. Temperature: 50-85 degrees. Pests: scale, mealybugs, edema.

**Janet Craig Dracaena** (*Dracaena deremensis 'Janet Craig'*). Light: medium to high. Temperature: 60-85 degrees. Pests: scale, spider mites.

**Marble Peperomia** (*Peperomia obtusifolia 'Marble'*). Light: medium to high. Temperature: 60-80 degrees. Pests: edema.

**Marble Queen** (*Scindapsus aureus 'Marble Queen'*). Light: medium to high. Temperature: 55-85 degrees. Pests: mealybugs, spider mites.

**Ming Aralia** or **Ming Tree** (*Polyscias fruticosa*). Light: high. Temperature: 60-85 degrees. Pests: aphids, mealybugs, thrips.

**Needlepoint Ivy** (*Hedera helix 'Needlepoint'*). Light: medium to high. Temperature: 55-80 degrees. Pests: scale and cyclamen mites.

**Norfolk Island Pine** (*Araucaria heterophylla*). Light: medium to high. Temperature: 55-85 degrees.

**Parlor Palm** (*Chamaedorea elegans 'Bella'*). Light: medium to high. Temperature: 55-85 degrees. Pests: spider mites, scale.

**Parsley Ming** or **Bonsai Aralia** (*Polyscias fruticosa 'Elegans'*). Light: high. Temperature: 60-85 degrees. Pests: aphids, mealybugs, scale, thrips.

**Peace Lily** (*Spathiphyllum 'Mauna Loa'*). Light: high. Temperature: 60-85 degrees. Pests: spider mites, scale.

**Red Emerald Philodendron** (*Philodendron x 'Red Emerald'*). Light: medium to high. Temperature: 60-85 degrees. Pests: virus, scale.

**Red-margined Dracaena** or **Madagascar Dragon Tree** (*Dracaena marginata*). Light: medium to high. Temperature: 60-85 degrees. Pests: spider mites.

**Red-veined Prayer Plant** (*Maranta leuconeura erythroneura*). Light: low to high. Temperature: 55-85 degrees. Pests: spider mites, mealybugs.

**Ribbon Plant** (*Dracaena sanderana*). Light: medium to high. Temperatures: 60-85 degrees. Pests: spider mites.

**Rubber Tree** (*Ficus Elastica 'Robusta'*). Light: medium to high. Temperature: 55-85 degrees. Pests: thrips.

**Schefflera** or **Umbrella Tree** (*Brassaia actinophylla*).

Light: high. Temperature: 60-85 degrees. Pests: spider mites, aphids, scale.

**Silver King Evergreen** (*Aglaonema 'Silver King'*). Light: low to high. Temperature: 65-85 degrees. Pests: scale, mealybugs.

**Snake Plant** or **Mother-in-law's Tongue** (*Sansevieria trifasciata 'Laurenti'*). Light: low to high.

**Spineless Yucca** (*Yucca elephantipes*). Light: medium to high. Temperature: 60-85 degrees. Pests: thrips.

**Sweet Boxwood** (*Sarcococca ruscifolia*). Light: medium to high. Temperature: 50-85 degrees. Pests: scale, mealybugs.

**Sweetheart Ivy** (*Hedera helix 'Sweetheart'*). Light: medium to high. Temperature: 55-80 degrees. Pests: scale, cyclamen mites.

**Tricolor Wax Plant** (*Hoya carnosa 'Tricolor'*). Light: medium to high. Temperature: 55-80 degrees. Pests: mealybugs, aphids, thrips.

**Variegated Chinese Evergreen** or **Silver Evergreen** (*Aglaonema commutatum elegans*). Light: low to high. Temperature: 65-85 degrees. Pests: scale, mealybugs, virus.

**Variegated Peperomia** (*Peperomia obtusifolia 'Variegata'*). Light: medium to high. Temperature: 60-80 degrees. Pests: virus.

**Warnecki Dracaena** (*Dracaena deremensis 'Warnecki'*). Light: medium to high. Temperature: 60-85 degrees. Pests: spider mites, scale.

**Wax Plant** or **Hoya** (*Hoya carnosa 'Rubra'*). Light: medium to high. Temperature: 55-80 degrees. Pests: thrips, aphids, mealybugs.

**Weeping Fig** (*Ficus benjamina*). Light: high. Temperature: 65-85 degrees. Pests: scale, thrips.

**White Zebra Plant** (*Aphelandra 'Silver Cloud'*). Light: high. Temperature: 55-80 degrees. Pests: spider mites, aphids, broad mites, thrips.

91

# Appendix

## Glossary . . . words to help you understand your plants

**Aerial root.** A root that grows out from the stem and extracts moisture from the air as differentiated from those that grow in water or soil. Ivies and other vining plants typically have aerial roots, in addition to those roots growing in Living Stones.

**Air-layering.** A propagation technique which lets you reduce the height of a plant that's grown too tall. Basically, you partially sever the trunk, wrap with damp sphagnum moss until roots form, then remove the upper segment and put it in a new pot. New growth should eventually sprout from the lower or remaining plant trunk or stem. For details, see page 49.

**Artificial light.** Certain wavelengths from fluorescent tubes and incandescent bulbs can supplement or entirely substitute for natural sunlight. See pages 24-25. Also check *grow-lights, natural light*.

**Bookings.** Signing up to host a future Deco Plant Party with a Deco Consultant. Hostesses can earn gift credits or specials as a results of bookings.

**Bright light.** The intensity within three feet of a south-, west- or east-facing window. Bright light should be filtered or indirect, though. Don't confuse it with full sunshine, which can burn leaves of most houseplants.

**Bud.** The portion of a plant from which a shoot, cluster of leaves or a flower develops.

**Capillary action.** The tendency of water or any other liquid to seek out the smallest possible space and to work its way up through small openings such as the spaces between Living Stones. To see capillary action, turn to page 17.

**Crawlers.** Baby insects that move about on plant surfaces.

**Cutting.** A plant leaf, tip or stem that's been cut off and is capable of developing into a new plant. Cuttings for the Deco Plantsystem are rooted in water. To learn about this propagation technique, see pages 42-49.

**Deco Consultant.** An independent business person who organizes Deco Plant Parties, demonstrates the Soilfree Deco Plantsystem and markets Deco products.

**Deco Plant Party.** A social event organized to spread the word about the Soilfree Deco Plantsystem. For more details, see pages 10 and 11.

**Direct light.** Full sun. Direct sunlight will burn the leaves of most houseplants.

**Dormant.** A rest period during which plant growth ceases or slows down. Most (but not all) plants are dormant in winter—from early in December to mid-February.

**Dwarf.** A plant that has the same characteristics of others in its genus and species, but consistently grows smaller. Many houseplants are dwarf versions of tropical trees.

**Force.** To make a plant bloom before the season when it naturally flowers. Warm temperatures, artificial light or other factors can "fool" a plant into thinking it's time to show off.

**Fungus.** Molds, mildew and other undesirable growths that can attack plants, usually under conditions that are very damp.

**Genus.** A broad class of plants that have similar but not identical characteristics. A plant's Latin name always gives its genus first. Also see species.

**Grow-lights.** Special fluorescent tubes or incandescent bulbs that emit the light rays plants need for healthy growth. Regular widespectrum fluorescents also may be used. To learn about grow-lights, see pages 24 and 25.

**Honeydew.** A sticky amber substance created by some insects—such as scale or aphids—as they feed on plant surfaces. Often it turns a moldy black and impedes transpiration.

**Hybrid.** A cross between two or more plants of different heritages, which usually produces a more vigorous plant. Many houseplants are hybrids.

**Hydroculture.** The technique of growing plants in water rather than soil. Sometimes called *hydroponics*. Also see *Soilfree Deco Plantsystem*.

**Indirect light.** Sunshine that's filtered or reflected. Almost all Deco Plants prefer indirect light; full sun can burn their leaves.

**Larvae.** Newly hatched insects, often wormlike in character.

**Leaching.** Flushing out any salt or chemical buildup that may have accumulated in your plants' Living Stones by using vigorously running lukewarm water. See page 26.

**Leggy.** Said of a plant that's tall, does not branch as it should, and often has almost all of its leaves clustered at the top. Usually caused by too little light or by lack of pinching or pruning growth back at the proper stages.

**Life cycle.** The series of stages an insect passes through, from egg to death. Since most eggs are immune to most pest controls, you usually must treat an infested plant at least two to three times at 7- to 10-day intervals to catch newly hatched pests. Pages 32 to 41 present the life cycles of most houseplant pests.

**Living Stones.** Lightweight synthetic aggregate that provides a support base for plant roots and gives them just the right amount of moisture. Along with *Nutrient Solution* and the *Visual Moisture Level Indicator*, Living Stones are one of the key ingredients of the *Soilfree Deco Plantsystem*.

**Low light.** The level that prevails in areas six to ten feet from a nonshaded east, west or south window. Some plants tolerate low light, but most do better in *medium light.*

**Medium light.** The level you get at three to six feet from any but a north window. More about light levels on pages 20 and 21.

**Misting.** Increasing humidity levels around plants by spraying their foliage with water. Misting helps new plants get acclimated to the Soilfree Deco Plantsystem. For more effective ways to increase humidity, see pages 28 and 29.

**Natural light.** Pure sunlight, either *direct* or *indirect.*

**Node.** The point on a stem from which a new leaf or stem will grow. Cut below the node and insert the node in water, and roots should develop.

**Nutrient Solution.** A scientifically balanced blend of fertilizer and water that eliminates the guess-work of when and how much to feed your Deco Plant. You pour it over the *Living Stones* to the depth indicated by the *Visual Moisture Level Indicator.*

**Offsets.** Short shoots that rise up next to a mature plant and can be used for propagation, as explained on page 49.

**Overfeeding.** Perhaps the number two enemy of soil-grown plants. Too much fertilizer and the victim dies from excess fertilizer salts which "burn off" functioning roots.

**Over-watering.** Perhaps the number one killer of soil-grown plants. All too often you don't realize they're getting too much moisture until roots begin to rot. Keep an eye on the *Visual Moisture Level Indicator* and you should never overwater a Deco Plant.

**Phototropic.** Describes a plant's natural tendency to grow toward its light source. Well-rounded plants should be rotated every few days or they'll begin to lean.

**Photosynthesis.** The action of light on the chlorophyll in plants that results in the plant making food.

**Pinching back.** To pinch off growth at tips of plants to encourage side growth to make a plant bushier.

**Propagation.** To increase plants by such methods as cuttings, division or air-layering, described on pages 42 to 49.

**Pruning.** Cutting back a plant for stronger, fuller growth. More drastic than *pinching back.*

**Rhizomes.** A type of elongated stem beneath the growing surface from which new shoots or plants arise.

**Rootbound.** When roots completely fill a pot. Rootbound Deco Plants grow out through the slits in their Planting Baskets and may fill the outer container.

**Root division.** A propagation technique that involves cutting or pulling apart the root systems of multi-stemmed plants. You end up with two complete, but smaller, plants. More about this on page 49.

**Rooting.** Take a leaf, stem or tip cutting and stick it in water, and soon a miniature root system will begin to take shape. Knowing this, you can propagate almost any houseplant with one of the techniques explained on pages 42 to 49.

**Root rot.** Besides water, roots also need air—which they get by drying out periodically. Keep roots constantly under water and you can drown a plant. This happens frequently in soil-based systems, although the Living Stones in the Deco Plantsystem help prevent this. For more about root rot, check pages 15 and 17. Also see *over-watering.*

**Soilfree Deco Plantsystem.** Three simple components put hydroculture in your home. Deco Plants grow in a base of *Living Stones* that use capillary action to nourish roots with *Nutrient Solution.* A *Visual Moisture Level Indicator* lets you add the correct amounts of water and food your plant needs.

**Species.** A particular plant within a *genus*, the second or last part of its Latin name. With *Aglaonema modestum*, for instance, *Aglaonema* is the genus, *modestum* the species.

**Succulent.** A plant, such as the Jade, that stores moisture in its plump, fleshy leaves. These don't need watering as often as other houseplants.

**Sunburning.** Exposing leaves to direct sun can turn them yellow, then brown. You may see spots on some, scorched edges and tips on others. For more about sunburn cases, see page 22.

**Tendril.** A slender, elongated leaf or stem that clings to a support as it grows. Ivies typically send out tendrils. Also see *aerial roots.*

**Training.** Entice vining plants with light, give them something to cling to, and they'll take almost any shape you like.

**Transpiration.** A plant's breathing process. Pores in its leaves give off moisture. Plants inhale carbon dioxide and exhale oxygen.

**Transplanting.** Removing a mature plant from its container and installing it in another. The Soilfree Deco Plantsystem makes this an easy task, so try it when a specimen becomes rootbound. You can transplant from soil to the Deco Plantsystem, too. Pages 46 to 49 show how to do it.

**Under-watering.** Less of a danger than over-watering. Always let the Visual Moisture Level Indicator drop to the minimum mark before adding fresh Nutrient Solution. Don't leave a plant dry for more than a few days, though, or it'll die of thirst.

**Variegated.** Foliage that has more than one color, giving it a dappled appearance.

**Visual Moisture Level Indicator.** The third key element in the Soilfree Deco Plantsystem. It tells exactly how much Nutrient Solution is in the reservoir at the base of the Living Stones. See pages 12 and 13, 14 and 15, 16 and 17.

# Index

95

# Index